CHARLOTTE FORTEN

A Black Teacher in the Civil War

Peter Burchard

Crown Publishers, Inc., New York

Library of Congress Cataloging-in-Publication Data
Burchard, Peter.
Charlotte Forten : a Black teacher in the Civil War / by Peter Burchard.
p. cm.
Includes bibliographical references and index.
1. Forten, Charlotte L.—Juvenile literature. 2. Afro-American teachers—Biography—Juvenile literature. 3. United States—History—Civil War, 1861-1865—Juvenile literature. 4. Afro-Americans—History—To 1863—Juvenile literature. 5. Afro-Americans—History—1863-1867—Juvenile literature. [1. Forten, Charlotte L. 2. Teachers. 3. Afro-Americans—Biography. 4. Women—Biography. 5. United States—History—Civil War, 1861-1865.]
I. Title.
LA2317.F67B87   1994
371.1'0092—dc20
[B]   94-18305
ISBN 0-517-59242-8   (trade)
ISBN 0-517-59243-6   (lib. bdg.)
10 9 8 7 6 5 4 3 2 1

First Edition

For my daughter Lee, with love

CONTENTS

1

"How wild and strange it seemed"

Shortly after noon on a bright October day in 1862, the steamship *United States* moved swiftly down the Hudson River toward New York Bay, taking Charlotte Forten on her first long sea voyage.

Charlotte was twenty-five, slim and graceful. Former slave William Wells Brown, who had known her as a schoolgirl, wrote that her face was "beaming with intelligence." Born into one of America's prominent black families, she was an educated woman.

In 1862 most of the buildings of New York stood on the rock and soil of the lower reaches of Manhattan, where the golden weathervanes of the city's tallest steeples rose above row after row of five-story red brick buildings. The masts and spars of a great variety of sailing ships and steam packets marked the country's largest seaport, and the bells and whistles of the waterfront could be heard from the decks of the departing steamer.

The ship that carried Charlotte toward the sea had sailed often to and from Germany, France, and England, but on that October day it was bound for Hilton Head, one of the Sea Islands, a chain of plantation lands and deserted sandy wastes off the coasts of Florida, Georgia, and South Carolina. These were islands separated from the mainland and from each other by salt marshes, rivers, creeks, and estuaries.

Charlotte's nation was involved in a far-ranging civil war—North against South—and as the fighting thundered onward in Maryland

and Virginia and along the Mississippi River, she was bound for South Carolina, the state where the first shot had been fired. She was going to the Port Royal region to educate the children of the slaves who had escaped or had been abandoned when soldiers from the North had landed on the islands in the fall of 1861. No important land battles had been fought in South Carolina, but nine months after her arrival there, black men in a Massachusetts regiment were to fight and die near Charleston.

The *United States* moved across the broad expanse of New York Bay. Charlotte, whose forefathers had been sailors, wrote later, "Enjoyed the sail down the harbor perfectly." Led by a pilot boat—a rugged sailing vessel—the *United States* moved through the Narrows, which was flanked on one side by the gentle hills of Brooklyn and on the other by the narrow Staten Island beaches. Off Sandy Hook the pilot boat turned back toward the bay while the steamship headed for the open sea.

At age sixteen Charlotte had begun to keep a diary. She wrote about

View of New York Harbor from Brooklyn Heights, 1860.

her changing moods, her friendships, and her work. She revealed the bitterness and anger of a sensitive black woman who was living in a time when slavery and prejudice were dividing her young country.

By the early nineteenth century, slavery had disappeared in all the northern states but was spreading in the South. Charlotte knew that four million slaves had been kept in ignorance. She understood that very few free black men and women in the North had been adequately educated, and aware of the many privileges she had enjoyed, she hoped that her writing—her essays and poetry—would command recognition and bring honor to her race. She never guessed that her journal, kept only for herself, would become more important than her other work.

Two months before leaving for Port Royal, on her twenty-fifth birthday, she had written, "Ten years ago, I hoped for a different fate at twenty-five. The accomplishments, the society, the delights of travel which I have dreamed of and longed for all my life, I am now convinced can never be mine. If I can go to Port Royal, I will try to forget all these desires."

It is strange that Charlotte thought that she had missed accomplishments and the company of interesting people. Five of her poems and one of her essays had been published. She knew many brilliant abolitionists—men and women working against slavery—and she counted as a friend John Greenleaf Whittier, one of the great poets of the nineteenth century.

At sea, Charlotte wrote, "Went below for the night into the close ladies' cabin....Was terribly sea-sick that night and all the next morning."

She and her companion, Elizabeth Hunn, who was going to Port Royal with her father to set up a store for the islanders, resolved to pass the next night in the open. Wrapped in shawls, lying on deck chairs, they spent a pleasant evening. Charlotte noted, "Two passen-

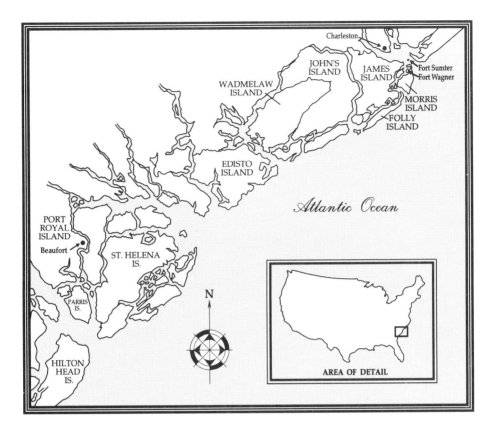

The South Carolina coast, from Charleston to the Port Royal region.

gers from Hilton Head, who were very gentlemanly and attentive, entertained us for some time with some fine singing, then retired." Left alone, the two young women talked awhile before they slept. "How wild and strange it seemed there on deck in the dark night, only the dim outlines of sea and sky to be seen, only the roaring of the waves to be heard....The thought that we were far, far away from the land was a pleasant one to me."

The next day Charlotte mixed with other passengers. As a child in Philadelphia she had been turned away from theaters, concert halls, museums, shops, and libraries. Always expecting prejudice, she encountered none at sea. "There was no difficulty as I feared there might be. People were as kind and polite as possible. Indeed I have had no trouble since I have been on board."

At meals she sat next to a New England sea captain who was pleasant company. "He is a Cape Cod man, had been to sea ever since he was nine years old. He had visited many lands and I enjoy hearing him talk about them."

On Charlotte's fourth day at sea, the weather changed. The sky was darkened by a horde of leaden clouds, thickening as they moved west, gathering, pushing upward. The vast waters of the deep were streaked and flecked with white.

Charlotte started to enjoy herself. "I am feeling well and *luxuriating* in the beauty of the sea and sky." That afternoon one of the young men from Hilton Head went with her as she staggered forward to the bow "and there saw the sea in all its glory and grandeur. Oh, how beautiful those great waves were as they broke upon the side of the vessel, into foam and spray, pure and white as new fallen snow."

That night, Charlotte walked around the deck and marveled at the phosphorescence "—the long line of light in the wake of the steamer—and the stars, and sometimes balls of fire that rise so magically out of the water."

On the day of her arrival in Port Royal, Charlotte wrote, "This morning Mr. Hunn came to our door to tell us that we were in sight of the blockading fleet at Charleston harbor." Charlotte and Lizzie Hunn "saw the masts of the ships looking like a grove of trees in the distance."

The Civil War had begun before sunrise on April 12, 1861, when the Confederacy, made up of states that had joined together to secede from the Union, fired on Fort Sumter, on an island at the mouth of Charleston harbor. Most federal forts in the South had surrendered to Confederate soldiers while Fort Sumter's Major Robert Anderson had remained steadfast. Following the bombardment,

Blockading Union warships off the Carolinas.

short of water, food, and ammunition, Anderson was compelled to surrender.

Shortly after war began, President Abraham Lincoln and his generals made plans to encircle the Confederacy. These plans included a blockade of Southern ports on the Atlantic and Gulf coasts and eventual control of the Mississippi River. The blockade was designed to keep France and England from exchanging guns and ammunition for the products of the South, especially the long-staple cotton that was grown in the Sea Islands. The blockading Union ships that Charlotte saw on that October morning were anchored out of range of the guns of Fort Sumter but were close enough to the channel so that they could fire on ships bound for Charleston.

The *United States* steamed southwest along bright beaches rimmed with surf and backed by groves of pine and live oak trees, overshadowed by palmetto trees. Here and there, the sails of a fishing boat ghosted white against the shadows of the undergrowth. Having spent several years on the New England coast, where the waters of the North Atlantic shattered against jagged rocks, Charlotte was disappointed in this southern coastline, but she noted optimistically that, in that season, oranges would be ripe in the islands.

Port Royal Sound served as an anchorage and headquarters for the blockading fleet so, at any given time, at least sixty vessels were moored in its protected waters—troop and cargo ships, steam frigates, gunboats, and assortments of flatboats, riverboats, and fishing boats. Charlotte noted, "Hilton Head looks like a very desolate place—just a long low sandy point running out into the sea with no visible dwellings upon it but the soldiers' white roofed tents."

The *United States* docked at the end of a long pier that extended outward from the north shore of the island, where army engineers had built sheds and warehouses—shelters for coal, lumber, food, and ammunition. As the ship approached the pier, Charlotte saw a horde of freed slaves, called contrabands. These people were barefoot, clothed in rags, or almost naked. Always sensitive to the condition of black people, Charlotte was shocked at their apparent poverty and lack of pride.

Late that afternoon, Charlotte and the Hunns stepped aboard the *Flora*, a riverboat capable of entering the surrounding shallow waters. The *Flora* crossed the sound, steamed along the shores of Parris Island, and moved up a narrow waterway to Beaufort, the only town of any size in the region.

A sandy street ran along the riverfront. Wide lawns, shaded by huge live oak trees hung with ribbons of gray Spanish moss, sloped upward to tall houses, most of which had belonged to wealthy planters but were now inhabited by contrabands and Union officers. One of them was occupied by Harriet Tubman, a determined black woman who had helped several hundred slaves escape to Canada, sometimes urging on fainthearted people with a loaded pistol.

In Beaufort, Charlotte and the Hunns waited in a ramshackle building on the waterfront for the flatboat that would take them to St.

Helena, the island where they were to live and where Charlotte was to teach. In the building they encountered several Union officers who pretended to ignore the newcomers and chattered foolishly among themselves, in loud voices. That night, Charlotte wrote in her diary that one of them "was a perfect popinjay, and he and a Colonel somebody who didn't look any too sensible, talked in a very smart manner, evidently for our special benefit. The word 'nigger' was plentifully used, whereupon I set them down at once as *not* gentlemen. Then they talked a great deal about enemy attacks and yellow fever, and other alarming things, with significant nods and looks at each other. If they are a fair example of army officers, I should pray to see as little of them as possible."

Charlotte, who had often been insulted in the North, was neither hurt nor surprised by the language of these men. Certainly, the officers failed to frighten either her or her companions, but Charlotte knew that, if captured, she might well become a slave—a fate she thought of as far worse than death itself.

At last the flatboat arrived. "To my great joy found that we were to be rowed by a crew of negro boatmen." Unlike the contrabands on the dock at Hilton Head, these men were magnificent—tall, slim, and muscular, like proud Watusi warriors. "The row was delightful. It was just at sunset—a grand Southern sunset—and the gorgeous clouds of crimson and gold were reflected in the waters below, which were smooth and calm as a mirror. Then as we glided along, the rich and sonorous tones of the boatmen broke upon the evening stillness. Their singing impressed me much. It was so sweet and strange and solemn. 'Roll, Jordan, Roll' was grand."

It was dark when the boat reached a landing in a narrow creek on St. Helena, but the passengers found a carriage waiting for them. With the sweet songs of the oarsmen echoing in memory, Charlotte was alert to the unfamiliar sounds and smells of her new home. She heard the beating of the wings of a large water bird and breathed in the aroma of the marshes.

Charlotte was to spend her first week in the islands at The Oaks, a dignified plantation house, headquarters of what was called the Port Royal Relief Association. As the carriage pulled up at the bottom of a set of wooden steps, she saw a young woman in the doorway, a small silhouette against the yellow lamplight in the hall.

Laura Towne was a stranger, but she greeted Charlotte as a friend. Towne, who was in her early twenties, had pink cheeks and a strong but pleasant face. She described herself as first an abolitionist, then a teacher. She had come from Pennsylvania to take charge of educating the children of the contrabands.

In the morning, in a dilapidated buggy that was to be lent to Charlotte, Towne drove the new teacher down a winding road, in the shadow of live oaks and pines, to a red brick Baptist church, where classes were being held until a proper schoolhouse could be built. "We went into the school, and heard the children read and spell. The teachers tell us that they have made great improvement in a very short time, and I noticed with pleasure how bright, how eager to learn many of them seem. The singing delighted me most. They sang beautifully in their sweet clear tones, and with that peculiar swaying motion which I had noticed before in the older people, and which seems to make their singing more effective. They sang one of their own hymns 'Down in the Lonesome Valley,' which is solemn and most beautiful. Dear children, born in slavery, but free at last! May God preserve to you all the blessings of freedom, and may you be in every possible way fitted to enjoy them. My heart goes out to you. I shall be glad to do all that I can to help you."

2

"Remember the poor slave as bound with him"

Charlotte was born in her grandfather's house in Philadelphia, Pennsylvania, on August 17, 1837. Her mother, Mary Woods, had a second child, a boy who died in infancy.

Mary Woods died in her twenties, when Charlotte was a child of three. The Fortens' minister, Daniel Alexander Payne, remembered that on her last day Mary Woods wanted to hold Charlotte, then asked that she be taken from her. "They brought her infant to the bed, which caused her to say, 'I have kissed my babe, put her away. The Lord will have mercy on her.'" Charlotte's father, Robert Bridges

Philadelphia, 1855.

Forten, who was thought of as a cold and distant person, wept at his wife's bedside.

During Charlotte's childhood, Philadelphia was a world of churches, factories, and town houses. It was ninety miles or so from the sea, but it lay between two rivers, the Schuylkill and the Delaware. The Schuylkill was too shallow to accommodate large ships and was lined with parks, gardens, and waterworks. The city's wharves were on the Delaware, which flowed south and became a tidal bay before it emptied into the Atlantic Ocean.

Black people made up almost 10 percent of the city's population. Most were quiet, law-abiding citizens, but they found the white population hostile. A visitor from England wrote, "Nowhere is the prejudice against black people stronger than in Philadelphia, 'the city of brotherly love.'"

Charlotte learned from her grandparents that her mother had been beautiful, gentle, loving, and intelligent. Later, when Charlotte read letters written by her mother, she expressed her sense of loss. "As I read the words penned by that dear hand, a strange feeling of tenderness, of sadness, of *loneliness* came over me, and I could not refrain from tears. Dear, dear mother whom I have scarcely known, yet so warmly love....My heart yearns for thee!"

Charlotte loved her father but was never close to him. Like other members of his family, he was a dedicated abolitionist. He had a scientific turn of mind, and as a boy, he had designed and built a telescope nine feet long, an instrument that was admired by professional astronomers. After Mary Woods died, he remarried and had other children. In her teens, Charlotte was to write, "I have known but little of a father's love. It is hard for me to bear....I can say with tears how very *hard* it is."

Charlotte loved her mother's sister, Annie, and took comfort from

James Forten, Charlotte's grandfather.

the women in her father's family—her grandmother and her aunts—but for her first five crucial years her grandfather, James Forten, was the most important person in her life. Sitting on his knee, she heard him tell about his childhood and his youth, about his work—as a sailmaker, abolitionist, and advocate of women's rights. Near the end of his life, though he was sick, he spent hours reading to her. What she knew of him and what she would learn about him later, from her grandmother and her favorite aunt, became a cornerstone of her strong yet gentle character.

James Forten, born in 1766, became a leader of his people. As a child, he went to a Quaker school. When he was seven, his father, who worked for sailmaker Robert Bridges, was killed when he fell from the yardarm of a ship anchored in the Delaware. Hard times followed. James worked after school in a grocery store and, two years later, quit school to work full time in the store to support his mother and his sister Abigail.

Young as he was, he understood why his country went to war with Great Britain. He celebrated Thomas Jefferson's Declaration of Independence, the document that proclaimed all people in the country equal under law. In the fifth year of the Revolutionary War, when he was fourteen, James joined the crew of the privateer *Royal Louis*, an armed vessel owned by Philadelphia patriot Stephen Decatur, Jr. James served as a drummer and a powder boy—an assistant gunner— until the *Royal Louis* was captured by the British warship *Amphyon*.

As a black prisoner of war, James had no rights whatsoever and might well have been sold to a Caribbean slave trader, but his supposed enemy, Captain Beasley, master of the *Amphyon*, was opposed to slavery. James was clever, charming, and entertaining, and he won the heart of Beasley and his son, who was sailing with his father. Beasley offered James a chance to sail with him to England, so he could escape confinement in a British prison ship and avoid the possibility of being sold. But, not wanting to be thought of as a traitor to his country, James refused.

The young patriot spent seven months as prisoner 4102 in the dark, foul-smelling dungeon of an anchored ship before he was traded for a British prisoner. He emerged from this ordeal thin and weak but soon regained his health and, after the war ended, went to England. In London he met men and women who had spent their lives working to abolish slavery, among them abolitionist Granville Sharp, who nine years earlier had won freedom for all slaves from other lands as soon as they set foot on British soil.

A year later, back in America, James went to work for his father's friend and employer Robert Bridges, at first sewing heavy canvas sails. Bridges was impressed with his apprentice's inventiveness and industry and, after seven years, made him foreman of the loft.

In 1798 Bridges sold his business to James Forten. By 1832 Forten was rich enough to move from a small wood frame building in Southwark, on the Philadelphia waterfront, to a substantial red brick house at 92 Lombard Street, where his children and grandchildren would be sheltered from the winter winds that blew across the Delaware. But no amount of money could protect his family from the dangers shared by all free black Americans.

In 1800 James Forten was outraged by the refusal of the U.S. Congress to repeal the first Fugitive Slave Act, passed in 1793, which provided for the capture and return of slaves who escaped from one state to another. In that year he became a dedicated abolitionist and, after that, spent more than forty years campaigning against slavery and against the suggestion that all black Americans, both slaves and free people, be returned to Africa.

Against laws unfair to black Americans, he wrote bitterly, "The dog is protected and pampered at the board of his master, while the poor African and his descendant, whether a saint or a felon, is branded with infamy." He went on to say that there would soon be laws authorizing the police to put in jail any black man "who dares to walk the streets without a collar on his neck!"

In the fall of 1830 Forten helped fund the publication of William Lloyd Garrison's *The Liberator*, which became the most important antislavery paper in America.

Three years before Mary Woods gave birth to Charlotte, riots erupted a few blocks from Independence Hall, where the Constitution had been signed. During the 1830s, Irish and German immigrants streamed into the great cities of the North—Boston, New York, and

Philadelphia—in great numbers, looking for employment and for housing. These people entered into competition with poor black Americans, the people lowest on the social scale. On a warm summer day in 1834, one of James Forten's sons, then a child, was assaulted in the street by a gang of young white men but somehow managed to escape from his attackers. In the same year, a mob of several hundred white men and their sons, armed with clubs, marched south from Independence Square toward a neighborhood where large numbers of black people lived. A local historian remembered, "They were joined by others, and all proceeded to places of amusement where many Negroes were congregated, on South Street." There the mob attacked unarmed black men and destroyed flimsy houses occupied by black people. At last, the police arrived and the rioters dispersed.

On two successive nights, as the rioting resumed, it was clear that it was highly organized. White people had been warned to leave lamps burning in their windows so their houses would be spared. "In this three-day uprising, 31 houses and two churches were destroyed and Stephen James, an honest, industrious colored man was killed."

Four years later, a year after Charlotte's birth, an eyewitness wrote that on the day of "the dedication of Pennsylvania Hall, which was designed to be a center of antislavery agitation, a mob, encouraged by the refusal of the mayor to furnish adequate police protection, burned the hall to the ground and the next night burned the Shelter for Colored Orphans at Thirteenth and Callowhill streets."

James Forten died on February 24, 1842. As he lost strength, he took his wife's hand in his and said softly, "I am going now. I feel a peace that passeth all understanding."

It was only later that Charlotte understood how important her grandfather had been, not only to herself and other members of her family but to black people everywhere. A reporter for the *Philadelphia*

Public Ledger wrote that central to James Forten's funeral was a great procession "numbering from three to five thousand persons, white and colored, male and female." At least half of the many mourners were white people. "Among the white portion were seen some of our wealthiest merchants and shippers, captains of vessels and others.... The deceased had the reputation of being strictly honest, liberal to a fault, of unvaryingly kind and courteous demeanor."

So generous had James Forten been to abolitionists like Garrison that he left very little money to his wife and children. But the members of his family knew where the money had been spent and they were proud of him and of themselves.

Charlotte grew up in a world of intelligent and enterprising women. In a poem "To the Daughters of James Forten"—published in *The Liberator* on September 3, 1835—John Greenleaf Whittier had celebrated Charlotte's aunts and offered them *"A brother's blessing with a brother's prayer."* Speaking at the first meeting of the American Anti-Slavery Society in Philadelphia, held in December 1833, her aunt Margaretta, then twenty-five years old, recited a long poem she had written. It began:

"Ye blessed few! who now have stood the storm
Of persecution...."

In a bold voice she proclaimed:

"DOWN WITH OPPRESSION! FREEDOM IN ITS STEAD!"

Margaretta never married. She devoted all her energies to educating children of her race, promoting women's rights, and campaigning to

Robert Purvis.

abolish slavery. Busy as she was, Margaretta became Charlotte's most important relative—a source of love, inspiration, and encouragement.

When she was eight, Charlotte's father remarried and left her with the other members of her family in the house on Lombard Street. So intense were Philadelphia's racial problems that the Fortens educated their children at home; when she was young, Charlotte had private teachers.

Charlotte's fear and hatred of the Philadelphia streets was counterbalanced by her love for the large and comfortable farmhouse owned by her aunt and uncle Harriet and Robert Purvis in nearby Bucks County. In good weather Charlotte walked to a pier near the foot of Lombard Street, went aboard a riverboat and traveled fifteen miles or so upstream to a landing, where a member of the Purvis family welcomed her and drove her up a narrow country lane to the farm. There, far away from the clatter of the city, she took long walks across the open fields and wooded hills, slept soundly, woke up early. She wrote about a day she spent with a cousin, a son of Robert Purvis. "A delightful day. Jumped into the hay wagon, drawn by two really handsome grey mules, and took a pleasant ride with Charley Purvis. The air, so pure and refreshing, did me much good. Dearly, dearly do I love the country."

Charlotte's uncle Robert loved her and talked to her as an equal. She returned his affection. Born in 1810 in Charleston, South Carolina, Purvis was the son of the granddaughter of a slave and an English cotton broker. He had a handsome, gentle face. His dark brown eyes revealed intelligence and depth of character.

When he was nine, Purvis moved north to Philadelphia with his parents and two brothers. His father died when he was sixteen, leaving his wife and children what, in those days, was a fortune. Robert's share was $120,000. He was a founder of the American Anti-Slavery Society and, as Charlotte's grandfather had done, gave large amounts of money to William Lloyd Garrison and other abolitionists to support antislavery campaigns and publications.

The Purvis house was a station on the Underground Railroad, a system used to help escaped slaves journey north to Canada, where slavery was illegal. In the house a trusted carpenter had built a secret room where fugitives could eat and sleep until it was safe for them to move along.

Back in the city, Charlotte was reminded constantly that black Philadelphians were outcasts. Later she wrote about a time when she and a black friend of hers were "*refused* at two ice cream saloons, successively. Oh how terribly I felt! It is dreadful! dreadful! I cannot stay in such a place."

"I would fight for liberty until death"

In the fall of 1853, when she was sixteen, Charlotte left Philadelphia to live in Salem, Massachusetts. She was enrolled in Higginson Grammar School, a private school for young women, named for the son of an early Salem minister.

With her aunt Margaretta she traveled to New York by rail and went alone to Boston on a steamboat. She was met in Boston by a friend, and from there it was only a short run to Salem, on the Boston and Maine railroad line.

In Salem, Charlotte lived with Charles and Amy Matilda Remond,

Salem, 1854.

who, like Charlotte's parents, had been born into the northeastern black elite, a network of successful and distinguished people living mostly in New England, New York, and Pennsylvania—all of them educated abolitionists.

Charles Lenox Remond was a short, commanding man. He stood straight and wore carefully tailored clothes. He was a brave and loyal abolitionist who had lectured in both England and America. Until the rise of Frederick Douglass, the greatest of black abolitionists, Remond had been thought of as the undisputed leader of his people. There were those who thought that he had been embittered by the rise of Douglass, but the members of his family had long known him as a tense, bad-tempered person.

Amy Matilda Remond was a loving woman who was soon to become a substitute for Charlotte's mother. Born in New York City, she was the daughter of antislavery minister Peter Williams, rector of the oldest black Episcopal church in the United States. She married Joseph Cassey, a successful Philadelphia businessman, and raised their five children on Lombard Street, in Philadelphia, near the Fortens. Widowed and remarried to Charles Remond, she moved to Salem. Her two older sons were independent, but her younger children had come with her.

In the Remonds' house at 9 Dean Street—now Flint Street—the Cassey children welcomed Charlotte. Sarah, who was twenty, became Charlotte's older sister. Charlotte soon grew fond of Henry, who was three years younger than she was, and Frank, who was nine, became a brother.

Salem, built on a peninsula projecting northeast into Massachusetts Bay, was a declining seaport. It had once been second only to the nearby port of Boston, but, in Charlotte's youth, weeds grew between its paving stones.

Charles Remond.

Almost from the first, Charlotte felt at home in Salem. Many Salem people were broad-minded. Before Salem ended segregation, in 1843, it had maintained a school for exceptional black children.

Fascinated as she was by history, Charlotte was aware of Salem's distant past. Settled in 1626, it was at first ruled by Englishman John Endicott, a small man with a pinched face and an explosive temper who waged war on the peaceful native population. During its early days, there were slaves in Salem, and in 1692 one of these, called Tituba, was accused of practicing witchcraft. Tituba was tried, convicted, and sentenced to be hanged—although she was later pardoned.

Salem in Charlotte's time was less frightening than it had been in 1692, but even in 1853 Massachusetts tolerated grave injustices. It was the home of earnest abolitionists, but these people were outnumbered.

Before Charlotte moved there, at least two fugitives from slavery had been found in Boston and recaptured. In February 1851 a man named Shadrack, a waiter in the Cornhill Coffee House, had been taken into custody and then rescued from the Old Courthouse. In the same year, a plan to rescue Thomas Sims from the courthouse had been foiled. Charlotte was soon to witness yet another such outrage, an event as inhumane as a witch-hunt.

On May 24, 1854, Charlotte wrote on the first page of a copybook with cardboard covers: "I wish to record the passing events of my life, which even if quite unimportant to others, naturally possess great interest to myself." In her first entry, she noted all the joys of spring. "How bright and beautiful are these May mornings! The air is so pure and balmy, the trees are in full blossom, and the little birds sing sweetly. I stand by the window listening to their

Charlotte Forten's introduction to her journal.

music, but suddenly remember that I have an arithmetic lesson which employs me until breakfast; then to school, recited my lessons, and commenced my journal. After lunch, practiced a music lesson, did some sewing, and then took a pleasant walk by the water. I stood for some time admiring the waves as they rose and fell, sparkling in the sun, and could not help envying a party of boys who were enjoying themselves in a sailing boat."

Her next entry told a tragic story. On May 25 she wrote, "Did not intend to write tonight but have just heard of something that is worth recording....Another fugitive from bondage has been arrested." Anthony Burns was a young slave who had escaped from his master, Charles F. Suttle, of Alexandria, Virginia. Burns spent two months free in Boston, then was captured.

Most Southern slaves were kept in ignorance so that they would be less likely to escape, but as a child Burns had learned to read and write. He was a gentle, timid man, but when he was in his teens he was brave enough to preach the Gospel to his fellow slaves. His own story of his voyage north, given after he was captured, must have been a disappointment to the abolitionists who were anxious to present him as a hero.

On March 26, 1854, Burns, leased out as a stevedore, was working on the waterfront. He grew tired and fell asleep on board a ship that took him out to sea. At sea he decided he liked freedom, and when the ship arrived in Boston he went ashore, found work in a clothing store on Brattle Street and slept in a black neighborhood, on a slope of Beacon Hill, where he could live without attracting the attention of the police.

Alone in Boston, Burns was homesick for his brother and his friends. He wrote a letter to his brother, who was also one of Suttle's slaves, giving no return address but saying something about Boston. He gave the letter to another black man who was bound for Canada, asking him to mail it there. It was postmarked in Canada, but Suttle opened it, guessed that Burns was still in Boston, and decided to pursue him.

The second Fugitive Slave Act, passed by the U.S. Congress on September 18, 1850, called for heavy penalties for anyone who helped a slave escape or interfered with the recapture of a slave. The provisions of the 1850 act enabled Suttle to hound Burns and, when he found out where he was, demand that he be arrested.

On May 24, as Burns was walking home from work, he was confronted by two police officers, acting under orders from a U.S. marshal. Burns, terrified, offered no resistance and was taken to the Old Courthouse and jailed in an upper room of the tall, imposing building.

While Suttle prepared his case, his opponents rushed to the defense of Burns. Tempers flared on both sides. Abolitionists, including black Bostonians, posted notices of a protest meeting to be held in a building that had been the scene of early Revolutionary gatherings:

A MAN KIDNAPPED—
A public meeting will be held at Faneuil Hall
this (Friday) evening, May 26,
at 7 o'clock, to secure justice for a man claimed
as a slave by a Virginia kidnapper...

At Faneuil Hall, minister and abolitionist Theodore Parker spoke in ringing terms to the people in the crowd. Parker was forty-three, a brilliant and dynamic man, with thinning hair, bright blue eyes, and large, expressive hands. In one of his sermons he had said, "The man who attacks me to reduce me to slavery, in that moment of attack alienates his right to life, and if I were the fugitive, and could escape in no other way, I would kill him with as little compunction as I would drive a mosquito from my face."

At the meeting in defense of Burns, Parker said that if there was

ets of Boston on our way to the depot, seeing the military as they rode
g, ready at any time to prove themselves the minions of the South."

urns was denied the right to be released on bail and to be tried by
ry. His guilt was determined at a hearing. On June 2 Charlotte
e, "Our worst fears are realized. The decision was against poor
s....Even an attempt at rescue was utterly impossible. The prison-
as completely surrounded by soldiers with bayonets fixed, a can-
paded, ready to be fired at the slightest sign."

fact, as Burns was taken to the wharf to be returned to slavery,
as surrounded by eight companies of artillery, with various field
, a cavalry battalion, a regiment of infantry, and several compa-
f militia and cadets. Charlotte wrote, "Oh! with what deep sor-
o we think of what will doubtless be the fate of that poor man,
he is again consigned to the horrors of slavery."

Alexandria a 100-gun salute was fired in honor of the triumph
Fugitive Slave Act, but there were those in the South who saw
se for celebration. The *Richmond Examiner* declared that the
which Burns was returned "was a mockery and an insult....A
re such victories, and the South is undone."

irginia, Burns spent five months in jail, where his hands and
e chained so tightly that the manacles and leg irons cut his
last he was purchased from his owner by Massachusetts abo-
s and returned to New England, where he lectured against
nd became a minister. Weakened by the cruelty of his impris-
he died when he was only twenty-eight.

otte summed up her bitterness at the treatment given Burns.
ned a government that was so cowardly that it assembled
ds of soldiers to satisfy the demands of slaveholders, to
f his freedom a man created in God's own image, whose
se is the color of his skin!"

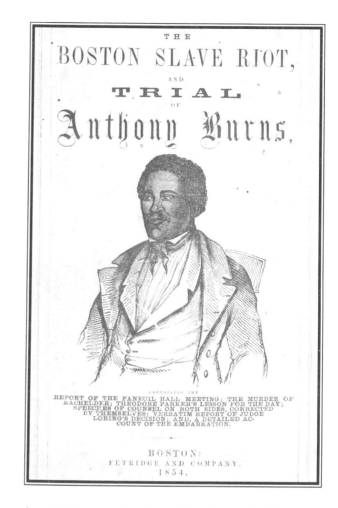

The cover of an 1854 pamphlet describing the trial of Anthony Burns.

any possibility of rescuing a man from slavery, he would act. "I am
ready to trample any statute or any man under my feet to do it."

Parker and his fellow abolitionists Wendell Phillips and Thomas
Wentworth Higginson, who was to become a friend of Charlotte's in
South Carolina, led a band of outraged men, including free black
Massachusetts citizens, toward the courthouse. Using a heavy beam
they battered down a door, and as they entered a hallway, someone
stabbed a marshal, killing him. The men were stopped before they
could rescue Burns, and after that authorities increased security in the

courthouse and the square. The murderer was never named. Some members of the party were charged with misdemeanors—minor violations of the law—but none of them was prosecuted.

While Burns was imprisoned in the courthouse, Charlotte went to Boston with her friend Sarah Cassey. Charlotte wrote, "Everything was quieter—outwardly—than we expected, but still much real indignation and excitement prevail. We walked past the courthouse, which is now lawlessly converted into a prison, and filled with soldiers, some of whom were looking from the windows, with an air of insolent authority, which made my blood boil, while I felt the strongest contempt for their cowardice and servility."

That afternoon the two young women went to a protest meeting and that evening to William Lloyd Garrison's town house on Dix Place, a narrow lamplit city street. Charlotte was impressed with Garrison, who was by then a famous abolitionist, and was charmed by his wife, Helen Benson, whose bright eyes and gentle smile put Charlotte at her ease. "Dined at the Garrisons'," she wrote. "His wife is one of the loveliest persons I have ever seen, worthy of such a husband."

Garrison was small, thin, and intense. In his youth he was poor. When he was in his early twenties, he lived in a rooming house in Boston, sometimes dining on no more than an apple and a single slice of bread. First he worked as a printer, then as a journalist, editor, and publisher. He often slept in his office, where he kept a cat, who was very fond of him. A friend remembered that the animal "caressed his bald forehead in a most affectionate way."

Garrison published several antislavery newspapers, one of which was called the *Genius of Universal Emancipation*. In 1830 he spent seven weeks in jail for libel, after accusing a New England shipper of transporting slaves from Baltimore to New Orleans. On January 1, 1831, he published the first issue of *The Liberator*. Four years later he was

William Lloyd Garrison.   *He*

mobbed by racists after speaking at a meeting o Slavery Society. He was seized and dragged rope was thrown around his body and the clotl

Charlotte and Sarah had supper at the about what was happening that week ir because he was nonviolent—expressed his d of the courthouse. Later Charlotte wrote earnestly the expression of that noble face the non-resistant principles to which he h his Christian spirit but did not agree wi believed "in resistance to tyrants, and I death."

After dinner Charlotte went with Sara home in the evening, and felt sick at he

stre
alon
B
a ju
wro
Burr
er w
non
In
he wa
pieces
nies o
row d
when
In
of the
no cau
way in
few mo
In V
feet we
flesh. A
litionist
slavery
onment
Charl
She scor
"thousar
deprive
sole offer

"For them the bright Christmas sun shines in vain"

The only black girl in her school, Charlotte reached out, sometimes almost desperately, for the friendship of the people she admired. Her schoolmates found her attractive, but not all were brave enough to cultivate her friendship. "I have met girls in the schoolroom and they have been thoroughly kind and cordial to me. Perhaps the next day, when I have met them on the street, they feared to recognize me. These I can but regard now with scorn and contempt."

Living on the shifting sands between childhood and maturity, she developed strong attachments. She loved Amy Matilda Remond and was especially fond of her teacher Mary Shephard, principal of Higginson. She waited every week for letters from her father, her grandmother, and her aunts.

As the spring of 1854 gave way to summer, she was cheered by the weather. "Another delightful morning, the sky is cloudless, the sun is shining brightly." But even on the best of days she remembered Burns, who was still in chains in Richmond. After noticing a robin in an apple tree behind the Remonds' house, she wrote that the bird's song "was far sweeter to me than the clearer tones of the canary birds in their cages, for they are captives, while he is free!"

Her father, who had thought of moving north, changed his mind. In her journal Charlotte wrote, "To my great disappointment, father has decided not to remove to New England. He is, as I feared he would be, much prejudiced against it on account of the recent slave case." In time, Robert Forten and his family went north to Canada, then to England, moves that further distanced him from his first child. He seldom wrote to Charlotte and, when he did, his letters sometimes went astray. But letters from her aunts and cousins raised Charlotte's spirits, and now and then her aunt Margaretta traveled north to visit her.

Mrs. Remond was a pianist, and Charlotte took piano lessons from her. Charlotte helped her with the housework, talked to her, and took comfort in her loving ways. They read to each other, sewed together, and took buggy rides in each other's company. Charlotte helped the younger children with their homework. In the nineteenth century, games like chess and checkers, amateur plays and concerts, and the forming of tableaux—dressing up and posing to create a pleasant picture—served as evening entertainments. Soon Charlotte began to feel that she was part of Mrs. Remond's family.

Charlotte loved Mary Shephard, but she couldn't quite embrace her pacifism. Charlotte wrote that, after school, they had "an hour's conversation about slavery and prejudice. I fully appreciate her kindness and sympathy with me. She wishes me to cultivate a Christian spirit in thinking of my enemies. I know it is right, and will endeavor to do so, but it does seem very difficult."

On days when she was snubbed by fellow students, she thought of England as a refuge. Her grandfather had told her about his stay in England, where he had been treated with respect, and she knew that England had long since done away with slavery. "I have seen today a picture of a dear old English church. How beautiful and picturesque it was with its ivy-wreathed spire and moss-covered walls.... Oh! England my heart yearns toward thee as to a loved and loving friend! I long to behold thee, to dwell in one of your quiet homes, far

Salem Common under snow.

from the scenes of my early childhood, far from the land—my native land—where I am hated and oppressed."

In Salem, Charlotte learned to ride horseback. She began one evening in the company of Sarah Cassey and Charles Remond, who was an expert horseman. That night Charlotte wrote, "It was my first experience with equestrianism and I enjoyed it exceedingly. All my pleasant anticipations were more than realized. We rode ten miles. The weather was delightful and I thought I had never seen the country look so beautiful. Sarah and I had a fine race, and returned home too much delighted to feel at all tired."

Charlotte was an almost constant reader and took pleasure in her closeness to the haunts of great literary figures. John Greenleaf Whittier, whose poetry and pamphlets had inspired many antislavery readers, lived with his sister on their farm in Amesbury, twenty miles north of Salem, on land that had been settled by their forebears in 1688. Charlotte read and admired the early novels and short stories of Nathaniel Hawthorne, who, like Whittier, was a handsome and attractive man. He had been born in Salem and was in the middle of a four-year stay in England. Charlotte wrote, "I have seen a portrait of

Hawthorne....He has a splendid head. That expansive brow bears the unmistakable impress of genius...." Charlotte had been deeply touched by Hawthorne's masterpiece, *The Scarlet Letter*, whose central character is the young and beautiful Hester Prynne, married to a man long separated from her, who gives birth to a baby girl and is made to suffer for her sin.

Many books that Charlotte read were works of antislavery propaganda. Her favorite was a novel—Harriet Beecher Stowe's *Uncle Tom's Cabin*, which had swept the country and the world. Stowe, a New Englander, had read almost every issue of *The Liberator* but had never called herself an abolitionist. Abolitionist or not, in her novel she depicts a cast of brutalized black characters. A year after publication, the book had sold 305,000 copies in the United States and many more overseas in English and in other languages. During the coming war, Stowe, a small, mild-mannered woman, would pay a call on President Lincoln, who looked down at her from his great height and said gently, "So this is the little lady who made this big war." Of course, Lincoln knew that Stowe hadn't struck the spark single-handed, but he knew that her book had made everyone aware of slavery, the root cause of the Civil War.

When Henry Cassey was fourteen and Charlotte seventeen, it was clear that Henry, a bright and handsome boy, found her attractive, and it wasn't long before their friends began to notice that they spent a lot of time together. Indeed they did, but Charlotte scoffed at the notion that they might become romantically involved. In fact, at first she treated his affection for her as a joke. Coming home from a walk, she found that he "had brought me a large branch of the fragrant locust, which, he assured me, he had risked his life in obtaining. I could not help smiling, thinking he had become extremely generous and self-sacrificing, while I told him that I could not prize too highly that which had been so dearly bought." Later, when they were both adults, they were to share a deep and abiding friendship.

When Charlotte was seventeen, Mary Shephard asked her to try her hand at teaching. "This afternoon I had a lesson in teaching. I heard the recitations of the third and fourth classes. We got along very pleasantly and one pretty, rosy-cheeked little girl told me afterward that she liked me *very* much for a teacher."

In school, her best friend was Lizzie Church. After leaving school to take a short vacation, Charlotte wrote of Lizzie, "I felt very sad to part with that kind friend, even for a few weeks. She gently reproved me, when we were parting, for not returning her embrace. I fear she thought me cold, but it was not so. I know not why it is that, when I think and feel the most, I say the least."

On Christmas morning 1854, Charlotte wrote, "The return of the season brings to my mind many recollections both sad and pleasing—thoughts of home and the happy family meetings we have had on this delightful day. I imagine that I can see grandmother's face as she listens to the voices of the little ones around her wishing her a 'Merry Christmas.' The busy preparations for the grand dinner, the display of Christmas gifts, the pleasant salutations—I think of them all....

"In many homes there is happiness but alas in many others there is sorrow. The suffering poor, the oppressed and down-trodden of the earth—their hearts are sad today. For them the bright Christmas sun shines in vain....A great work lies before us to alleviate their condition, to make their lives brighter and happier that they, too, may enjoy this and every other gladsome season."

A month or so after Christmas a great snowfall blanketed the little city, covering Salem Common—a large green, roughly triangular, surrounded by stately houses. "A great quantity of snow has fallen, and very beautiful it looks in the bright sunlight....This afternoon had a sleigh ride, the first I have had this season."

In March, Charlotte graduated. Following examination day, she wrote of Mary Shephard, "I can scarcely bear to think how very soon I shall have to leave her."

A composition of Charlotte's, called "A Parting Hymn," was sung at the graduation ceremony. A friend wrote what is probably a fanciful account of the occasion. "After the singing of the hymn the principal said, 'Ladies and gentlemen, the beautiful hymn just sung is the composition of one of the students of this school....Will the author step forward?'

"A moment's silence, and every eye was turned in the direction of the principal." Mary Shephard was said to have repeated her request, and at last Charlotte rose and went forward to the platform. "Thunders of applause greeted the announcement that the distinguished authoress then before them was Charlotte Forten."

In the same month, Charlotte's first published poem appeared in *The Liberator*. It was dedicated to William Lloyd Garrison, who had referred to his struggle against slavery as his ruling passion, as his "Chosen Queen." In the poem, she expressed an altered view of Garrison's nonviolent principles. She wrote in part:

> *Thou, who so bravely dost her battles fight,*
> *With truer weapons than the blood-stained sword,*
> *And teachest us that greater is the might*
> *Of* moral *warfare, noble thought and work.*
> *On thee shall rest the blessing of mankind*
> *As one who nobly dost the right defend.*

Always modest, Charlotte signed herself C.L.F. and was annoyed when her aunt Margaretta recognized her signature. Thinking little of

The Liberator.

her poem, Charlotte noted, "If ever I write doggerel again, I shall be careful not to sign my own initials."

Charlotte knew that she had to earn a living and decided to prepare to be a teacher. She wasted no time in enrolling in the Salem Normal School—now Salem State College—which had opened only five months earlier. She had spent no more than a week at Salem Normal when she received an unwelcome letter from her father.

Charlotte had no money of her own, and her father had suddenly decided that he couldn't keep on paying her tuition at the school. "To my great surprise, received a letter from father summoning me to return home as soon as possible. I feel deeply grieved; it seems harder than ever to leave now that I have entered on a course of study which I so earnestly hoped would thoroughly qualify me for the duties of a teacher."

5

"She is gone!"

Richard Edwards, the principal of Salem Normal School, was a gentle, kindly person, with soft eyes and a pleasant smile. A deeply sympathetic man, he saw Charlotte's problem as his own. "This morning Mr. Edwards came to see me, and told me that he had no doubt of my being able to obtain a situation as a teacher here if I went through the Normal School. He wishes me to write to father and assure him of this."

Mary Shephard also wrote to Charlotte's father, telling him that she would willingly lend Charlotte money to continue with her studies. After she and Charlotte mailed their letters, Charlotte noted, "I have found it almost impossible to concentrate my mind upon my studies which, though difficult, would be interesting to me, were it not for the anxious, troubled thoughts which *will* intrude...."

Rescued from uncertainty by another letter from her father, in which he said that she could stay through her first term, she was delighted at the prospect of applying herself to the humanities—history, literature, philosophy, and the arts—but expressed less interest in the sciences and the people who taught them. "Colburn, the mathematician, visited the school today. His only remarkable feature is a very large nose which somebody says is a necessary appendage to all great men."

Sarah Cassey left the Remond household when she married a young man named Watson Smith, but it wasn't long before Sarah's husband died and she returned to 9 Dean Street. Sympathizing with her friend, Charlotte wrote, "Poor Sarah is far more to be pitied than he who has gone where suffering is unknown." Two days later she

Richard Edwards.

wrote about the funeral. "A very lovely but sad day. I have seen the remains of Mr. Smith consigned to their last resting place." She wrote that Sarah "suffers deeply. I know of no real consolation to hearts so deeply wounded...."

On July 4, thinking always of Americans in bondage, Charlotte echoed Garrison as she scorned displays of fireworks. "The *patriots*, poor fools, were celebrating the anniversary of their vaunted *independence*. Strange that they cannot feel their own degradation...."

Prominent in Salem's black community were members of the Putnam family. George and Jane Putnam occupied an enormous house at 9 Oak Street, across the North River from 9 Dean Street. They and their children and their friends welcomed Charlotte's company. Son Joseph and his wife Caroline were especially kind to Charlotte, and she often walked across the Carlton Bridge and crossed a set of railroad tracks to visit them.

In September, Charlotte went back to the Normal School. Sensitive, easily hurt, she imagined that most of her fellow students kept their distance. "There is one girl and only one—Miss Sarah Brown—who I believe thoroughly and heartily appreciates antislavery, *radical* anti-slavery, and has no prejudice against color."

With her own people and with sympathetic white friends, Charlotte could relax, but when she felt the sting of prejudice she grew bitter. Referring to black people in America, she remarked, "Surely we have everything to make us hate mankind...." Then, adding a determined, optimistic note, she wrote, "Let us take courage, never ceasing to work, hoping and believing that, if not for us, for another generation there is a better brighter day in store, when slavery and prejudice shall vanish before the glorious light of Liberty and Truth, when the rights of every colored man shall every-where be acknowledged and respected, and he shall be treated as a *man* and a *brother*."

Later in September, Charlotte noted, "This evening, Miss Sarah Brown and I joined the Female Anti-Slavery Society. I am glad to have persuaded her to do so. She seems an earnest-hearted girl, in whom I cannot help having some confidence. I can only hope and pray that she will be true and courageous enough to meet the opposition which every friend of freedom must encounter."

On January 1, 1856, Charlotte wrote, "The first day of the New Year, and Nature wears a robe of spotless white in honor of his birth. Those nations whose *mourning* robes are white would say that she laments the death of the *old*, instead of rejoicing at the birth of the new." Sad to say, the new year was to bring great sorrow to the house at 9 Dean Street.

As spring came around again, Charlotte was convinced that she could not afford to stay on at Salem Normal, but although at first her father withheld help, he did at last agree to pay part of her tuition and she borrowed money once again, hoping that, in working as a teacher, she could meet her obligations.

Approaching graduation, she wrote enthusiastically, "The days of my New England school life, though spent far from home and early friends, have still been among the happiest of my life. I have been fortunate enough to receive the instruction of the best and kindest teachers; and the new friends I have made are warm and true."

The Liberator, published every Friday, covered all the major antislavery gatherings and contained the texts of most speeches given by the country's leading abolitionists, including those of U.S. Senator from Massachusetts Charles Sumner, who was one of Charlotte's heroes. Charlotte had heard Sumner speak, had followed his career, and, in *The Liberator*, read about what happened to him on May 22, 1856. On May 19 and 20, he delivered an oration, in which he referred to a speech made earlier by U.S. Senator from South Carolina Andrew Pickens Butler who, as it happened, wasn't on hand to reply. Sumner stated flatly that South Carolina was disloyal to the Union. Criticizing Butler, he said in part, "The Senator dreams that he can subdue the North....How little that Senator knows himself or the strength of the cause he persecutes! He is but mortal man; against him is an immortal principle. With finite power, he wrestles with the infinite, and he must fall. Against him are the invincible sentiments of the human heart; against him is God."

Two days later, Butler's nephew, Congressman Preston Brooks, a tall, physically imposing man, found a way to answer Sumner's speech. The event was reported in *The Liberator*.

ATTEMPT TO MURDER HON. CHARLES SUMNER

WASHINGTON, MAY 22. Shortly before two o'clock this afternoon, the Senate having adjourned, Mr. Sumner was sitting in his place writing very busily. Preston Brooks, of S.C., approached him saying, "Mr. Sumner, I have read your speech twice. It is a libel on South Carolina, and on Mr. Butler, who is a relative of mine." Brooks struck him with a heavy cane, upon which Sumner sprung up from his seat to defend himself, with such violence that the heavy desk before him was wrenched from the floor....He was, however, so much staggered as to be rendered powerless, and the blows were repeated until he was senseless. The two cuts upon his head are each about two inches in length and very deep.

His clothes soaked in his own blood, Sumner was taken from the Senate chamber to a room where he could be attended by a doctor and then moved to his home, where he began a three-year recovery. Brooks was never prosecuted for his crime. He resigned, but—a hero to the voters of South Carolina—he was promptly reelected.

For Charlotte, this disturbing evidence of her country's drift toward war was balanced by good news in Salem. A month before she graduated from the Salem Normal School, Richard Edwards summoned her. "Amazing, wonderful news I have heard today! It has completely astounded me. I cannot realize it. Mr. Edwards called me into his room with a face full of such grave mystery that I at once commenced reviewing my past conduct....The mystery was most pleasantly solved." Edwards told her that the principal of the Epes Grammar School, a Salem public school, had offered her a position on his teaching staff. "Wonderful indeed it is!" Knowing that Edwards must have recommended her, she added, "I thank him with all my heart."

Charles Sumner.

At her graduation ceremonies, on July 22, Charlotte read a poem she had written celebrating the occasion. It was later published in *The Liberator*. At last she began to believe that she had a future as a writer and a teacher.

In July and during part of August, Charlotte spent most of her time taking care of Amy Matilda Remond, who was suffering from an unidentified disease—probably tuberculosis. Charlotte and Sarah Cassey did everything they could to make the older woman comfortable. Charlotte wrote, "Our beloved patient grows worse. She cannot endure this terrible oppressive heat. Oh! How much these weeks of illness have changed her. As I gaze upon her, lying on her bed of suffering, I can scarcely realize that it is indeed she who, a few short months ago, seemed in such perfect health and spirits. Dear, dear friend, I earnestly, fondly hope that she will recover."

In early August, when her patient was no better, Charlotte wrote, "Every moment that I can spare I devote to her. All that love and care can do is done for her, I fear in vain. Still there is *some* hope."

Amy Remond died on August 15. "All is over! This morning, between four and five, the dearly loved one passed away from us.... The nurse and I sat with her through the night." Charlotte lamented, "She is gone! Peacefully, without a murmur, she passed away. The loveliest of women, the best and kindest of friends to me. *Her* place can never be filled."

The day after the funeral, Charlotte voiced her sadness once again. "My nineteenth birthday—the saddest I have ever known." She noted that the Garrisons came from Boston to attend the funeral. In a rush of sympathy for Sarah, who had lost first her husband, then her mother, Charlotte wrote, "Poor dear Sarah, I pity her; she has had many trials for one so young."

In October, Charlotte went to a lecture by Richard Henry Dana, Jr., anti-slavery activist and author of *Two Years Before the Mast*, the story of the hardships he endured as an ordinary seaman, published sixteen years before. Tightly knit and immensely energetic, Dana had long hair, conspicuous sideburns, and a gaze that seemed fixed on far horizons. Though he had fought against the Fugitive Slave Act of 1850, he was a moderate, believing that slavery should be kept from spreading into Western territories but that, where it existed, it should be abolished slowly.

Dana spoke about what was happening in Kansas Territory. The Kansas-Nebraska Act had been passed on May 30, 1854, while the uproar over Burns was in progress. The act left decisions about slavery to the settlers themselves. Passage of the act encouraged the proslavery settlers in Missouri, where slavery was permitted, to move to Kansas Territory so that Kansas, when admitted to the Union, would become a slave state.

In response to this strategy, abolitionists from the Northeast went west, most of them to Lawrence, Kansas, a free-state stronghold that had been established by the New England Emigrant Aid Company. John Greenleaf Whittier praised these people in a song called "The Kansas Emigrants," written in 1854:

> *We go to rear a wall of men*
> *On Freedom's southern line,*
> *And plant beside the cotton tree*
> *The rugged Northern pine!*

As Dana spoke, Kansas Territory was controlled by proslavery thugs, called Border Ruffians. These men rigged elections, plundered farms and villages, and terrorized and murdered settlers who were working to keep Kansas free. Under a provision of a law passed in the territory, settlers found with antislavery writings could be hanged. A journalist explained the law in simple terms. "The man who possesses a copy of *Uncle Tom's Cabin* is no better than a murderer."

The federal government was less than useless in protecting free-state settlers. In fact, President Franklin Pierce gave wide support to laws enacted by proslavery settlers, laws enforced under constant threats of violence.

On May 23, 1856, Border Ruffians attacked and destroyed the town of Lawrence and drove out its citizens—men, women, children—and, with two pieces of artillery, leveled the Free State Hotel. They attacked the offices of an antislavery newspaper, *Herald of*

Bust of John Brown.

Freedom, destroying the printing presses, scattering the type, and, at last, setting fire to the building.

Probably unknown to Dana, abolitionist John Brown, whom Dana had met years before, had responded to the raid on Lawrence. Thin and sinewy, with a nose like a hawk's bill, Brown was captain of a free-state settlement at Osawatomie, thirty miles south of Lawrence. A brooding and explosive man, he set out to make an example of a family of proslavery settlers, becoming what he called "an instrument in the hand of God."

In a wagon packed with guns, freshly sharpened swords, food, and camping gear, Brown, four of his sons, and three comrades traveled north. Late on the evening of May 24 he and his party took up their swords and walked quietly to a cabin occupied by Pleasant Doyle, his wife, and three sons, who were unarmed and owned no slaves. Doyle's third son, John, sixteen at the time, remembered later, "They came into the house, handcuffed my father and two older brothers and started to take me, but my mother begged them to leave me as I would be all the protection she would have." Brown and his men took Doyle and his two older sons to a grassy knoll some distance from the house and killed and butchered them. That same night Brown went on to butcher two more settlers.

In 1856 news traveled slowly, and in the succeeding weeks the details of the sack of Lawrence were reported piecemeal in *The Liberator* and in other papers, but *The Liberator* failed to mention John Brown's retaliation. Only after Brown's raid on the U.S. arsenal at Harpers Ferry, three years later, and his death on the gallows, were the earlier killings widely publicized.

Charlotte praised Dana's lecture and expressed a degree of sympathy for the antislavery emigrants in Lawrence but commented, "the poor slave for centuries has suffered tenfold worse miseries....I am glad that *something* has aroused the people of the North at last."

On New Year's eve, Charlotte thought again of Mrs. Remond. "The clock strikes twelve! The year has gone! Dear, dear friend, who has gone before us....May I ever remember thy beautiful example."

6

"*A soldier in the army of the Lord*"

"Salem. January 1, 1857. Welcome in, New Year!"

Though Charlotte welcomed the new year, she found it hard to rise above discouragement. She missed Amy Matilda Remond desperately, and Charles Remond, never cheerful, made life at 9 Dean Street less than pleasant. Charlotte longed to see her father. "Still no news from Canada. It grieves me deeply that father should act so strangely. It seems as if my only parent has quite forsaken me. I lay awake all last night thinking about it, and could not help crying. I wish he *would* write to me."

One night, at George and Jane Putnam's house, talk around the supper table turned to race relations. Joseph Putnam thought that Charlotte was too sensitive and told her so, but back in her room alone she wrote that her people were outcasts "from the rest of mankind....To me it is *dreadful, dreadful*. Were I to indulge in the thought I fear I should become insane. But I do not despair. I *will* not despair, though *very* often I can hardly help doing so. God help us! We are indeed a wretched people. Oh, that I could do much toward bettering our condition. I will do *all*, all the *very little* that lies in my power, while life and strength last!"

At last, on May 4, she had a letter from her father. "Came home from school *very* weary, and found, to my joyful surprise, a letter from father....He says he has written several times and has not heard from me. 'Tis very strange. He thinks of going to England or

Scotland! If so, I shall go. But I must not anticipate. It would be too delightful." Her father was a truthful man, and no doubt his letters had somehow gone astray, but though he did go to Britain, Charlotte never went with him.

In Salem, old sea captains sat together in the customhouse, their chairs propped against the yellowed walls, swapping stories of the China trade before the War of 1812. The wharves were rotting, but ships were still being built in Salem. On a bright May morning Charlotte went to Derby Wharf, to watch a launching at a nearby yard. Ships ready to be launched were strung with signal flags, and christenings were accompanied by the music of brass bands, long speeches, and the breaking of bottles of champagne across the bows of the new vessels.

Charlotte saw the launching, the first she had ever seen, from a distance. "We had a pleasant seat on some rocks projecting far into the water." She commented on the many pleasure boats whose owners had come out to see the colorful proceedings. "Very beautiful the white sails looked in the distance, skimming over the blue waters of the bay; and occasionally a graceful little vessel came near us, cleaving the waves as she glided swiftly along. The delightful, ever welcome, sea breeze greatly strengthened and refreshed me."

While she was still in her teens, a disease that was often found in black people and their polar opposites, light-skinned blonds, began to appear in Charlotte. She referred to it as lung fever, but it was undoubtedly a form of tuberculosis, which is caused by a bacillus that was not identified until 1882. Then, as now, it could act swiftly or vanish altogether. This was probably the disease that killed many members of the black community, including Charlotte's mother, Amy Matilda Remond, and Sarah Cassey's husband, and was soon to claim other friends and relatives. No wonder Charlotte thought that she might die before she had a chance to prove herself.

Lung disease sometimes forced her to go home to Pennsylvania. There, much as she loved her aunt Margaretta and the members of the Purvis family, she missed Salem, wrote often to her Massachusetts friends, and was always happy to return to her adopted state.

Back in Salem after one such visit, Charlotte's greatest hero came to pay a call on her. When she was told that she had a visitor, she "went wondering who it *could* be, and found Whittier!" He was an old friend of her family, but Charlotte was almost overcome at the appearance of the legendary poet in the house where she was living. Tall and dark, Whittier had an electric personality. Charlotte wrote, "A great and sudden joy has completely dazzled—overpowered me. I stood like one bewildered before the noble poet. My heart was *full* but I *could* not speak, though constantly tormented by the thought that *he* would think me stupid, very foolish; but, after a few simple words from him, I felt more at ease and, though I still could say but very little, it was a pleasure to listen to *him*. First we spoke of my old home and my present home. He asked me if I liked New England and it was such a pleasure to tell him that I loved it. Well to see the approving smile, the sudden lightning of those earnest eyes!"

A lifelong Quaker, Whittier was a dedicated pacifist. Only once was he to watch soldiers marching off to war—in the spring of 1863, when young Robert Gould Shaw led the first Northeastern regiment of free black men down Beacon Street, in Boston. Even then, Whittier refrained from expressing his emotions "lest I should indirectly give a new impulse to war." It was only later that he wrote, "I can never forget the scene as Colonel Shaw rode at the head of his men. The very flower of grace and chivalry, he seemed to me beautiful and awful, as an angel of God come down to lead the host of freedom to victory." Both Whittier and Shaw were to play important parts in Charlotte's life.

John Greenleaf Whittier.

Charlotte must have known how many women had adored John Greenleaf Whittier. Some had sent him snippets of material from the hems of their skirts and begged him to give them samples of his hair, but he had written about women, "I love to watch their airy motions and catch the dark brilliancy of their fine eyes...but trust me my heart is untouched."

After putting Charlotte at her ease, Whittier affirmed his belief in Quakerism—his conviction that divine truth could be found in the light of one's own heart. Before she went to bed that night, Charlotte wrote, "I shall never forget how earnestly, how beautifully the poet expressed his *perfect faith*, that faith so evident in his writing.

"At his request, I took him to see Miss Shephard. The joy and surprise were almost more than she could bear. I stayed but a little while and then left them together....This day is to be marked with a white stone."

* * *

Eventually, Charles Remond grew so cantankerous that Charlotte, Sarah, and the Cassey boys moved across the river to the Putnams' house. As Charlotte packed her things, she noted that without Mrs. Remond the house had "changed, so changed! Dear lost friend, I shall never forget thee—never!"

Though her life was happier at the Putnams', her health began to fail again. In February 1858 she wrote, "Au désespoir today. Wrote a *desperate* little note to Miss Shephard. I think I must go home." A day later she came close to a decision. "Constantly, I ask myself 'Am I doing right?' Yet I *believe* I am. If I entirely lose my health *now* of what use will my life be to me? None. I shall only be dependent....I would ten thousand times rather die than that."

As she left for Philadelphia, Charlotte had no way of knowing that she would overcome her illness, travel south in time of war, and take part in the first serious attempt to educate and rehabilitate a people born to slavery.

Until the fall of 1859, when she returned to Salem to teach again at Higginson, Charlotte lived in Pennsylvania. At 92 Lombard Street and at her aunt and uncle's farm, she went on with her studies, reading widely, playing the piano, writing poetry.

Her poem "Flowers" was accepted by the *Christian Recorder*. For the work, she was paid a dollar, the first money she had earned from writing.

She spent the summer months in Bucks County. On clear evenings she went out to the veranda. "I sat on the piazza, and tried to read but, if the birds had entered into a conspiracy to prevent me, they could not have been more successful...." Two little wrens were nesting in an evergreen. "I suppose they were adding some finishing touches to their dwelling. How busy and important they were!

"Bluebirds and occasionally a splendid, brilliant oriole alighted for a moment on the lawn—bright wings flashing like gems in the fading sunlight—then vanished. But what gladdened my eyes most was a pair of tiny humming birds—the most *jewel*-like of all the birds—who were playing at hide-and-seek amid the clustering leaves of the woodbine."

As she grew stronger, Charlotte wrote more poetry. In "Angel's Visit," her mother's face appears before her. Charlotte hears her voice and seems to feel "her cooling touch." In the fifth verse, Charlotte asks her mother for her blessing:

> *O, guide and soothe thy sorrowing child;*
> *And if 'tis not His will*
> *That thou shouldst take me home with thee,*
> *Protect and bless me still;*
> *For dark and drear had been my life*
> *Without thy tender smile,*
> *Without a mother's loving care,*
> *Each sorrow to beguile.*

Years before Charlotte's journal saw the light of day, black abolitionist and writer William Wells Brown wrote about "Angel's Visit" and its author: "In some of her other poems she is more light and airy, and her muse delights occasionally to catch the sunshine on its aspiring wings. Miss Forten is still young and has a splendid future before her."

Despite such encouragement, Charlotte sometimes gave voice to a wild impatience. "Tuesday, August 17. My birthday. Twenty-one today! It grieves me to think of it—to think that I have wasted so many years." Not long before, she had written, "I have read an immense quantity, and it has all amounted to nothing, because I have been too indolent and foolish to take the trouble of *reflecting*."

In the country, Charlotte had time for reflection, but when she returned to Philadelphia, she encountered stark realities. There, she was faced repeatedly with racial prejudice.

In 1859, in February, she wrote, "Heard today that there has been another fugitive arrested." Daniel Webster Dangerfield, a resident of Harrisburg, Pennsylvania, had been living peacefully with his wife and children when he was arrested in a farmer's market. He was sent to jail in Philadelphia, pending trial. Charlotte wrote, "God grant that the poor man may be released from the clutches of slave hunters." She added, "How long, oh, how long shall such a state of things as this last?"

Soon the question was resolved. "Good news! After waiting with intense and painful anxiety for the result of the three days' trial, we are at last gladdened by the news that the alleged fugitive, Daniel Dangerfield, has been released."

The resolution led to celebrations in the black community. "Friday, April 8. Long, long to be remembered. This evening attended a large Anti-Slavery meeting at Samson Hall, celebrating Daniel Dangerfield's release." The meeting had barely begun when the hall was invaded by a crowd of proslavery demonstrators. "They created a great disturbance, stamping, halooing, groaning etc. so that it was impossible to hear a word that the speakers were saying." The president of the society made an effort to restore order, but "the tumult increased every moment and at one time there was a precipitate rush forward. We thought we should be crushed, but I did not feel at all frightened. I was too excited to think of fear.

"The veterans in the cause said that it reminded them of the time when the new and beautiful Pennsylvania Hall—which was afterward burned to the ground—was mobbed."

The outcome gave Charlotte hope for Philadelphia. After the

police arrived, "Many of the disturbers were arrested, and order restored." At last, Robert Purvis, Charlotte's uncle, rose to speak. "His speech was fine, decidedly the most effective."

After the celebration, Charlotte went with him to Bucks County. Given the importance of the Purvis farm as a stop on the Underground Railroad, it was not surprising that Dangerfield took refuge there. "The hero of the last few days came here tonight. He is a sturdy, sensible seeming man. It makes my heart beat quickly to see one who has just had so narrow an escape from a doom far darker and more terrible than death. Nor is he quite safe yet, for we hear that there are warrants for his re-arrest. Poor man! There can be no rest for his weary feet nearer than the free soil of Canada. We shall be obliged to keep him very close." Two weeks later, Charlotte noted, "Dangerfield has left us and we hear with joy that he is safe in Canada. Oh, stars and stripes, that wave so proudly over our *mockery* of freedom, what is your protection!"

With the help of Robert Purvis, Dangerfield's wife and children also found their way to Canada, where they lived in peace with him until slavery was abolished.

In September, back in Salem, Charlotte lived at the Putnams' house and taught again at Higginson. She missed Joseph Putnam, who had died in January, but her friendship with his wife, Caroline, and other Salem friends matured and flourished.

War clouds had been gathering during all the years of Charlotte's childhood and youth. The advance of slavery into Western territories, the spread of violence on the Kansas and Missouri border, the enforcement of the Fugitive Slave Act of 1850, the Supreme Court decision of 1857 in the complicated Dred Scott case—in which a majority of justices declared that black people had no rights as citizens—and John Brown's raid on Harpers Ferry brought war ever closer.

Not long after Brown's murderous activities in Missouri, he had hatched a strategy for setting off a chain of slave revolts in the South. There had been slave uprisings—notably Nat Turner's insurrection in 1831—but Brown envisioned widespread revolution. He viewed the Appalachian Mountain Range, stretching from Maine to the Alabama border, as a spear that could be driven through the heart of slavery. He planned to start his campaign at the U.S. arsenal at Harpers Ferry, Virginia. There he hoped to capture arms and ammunition and move south, attracting slaves who would join what he hoped would become a large liberating army.

When Brown explained his plan to Frederick Douglass, Douglass said that Brown's first moves would command wide attention and that federal troops would corner him. Ignoring Douglass, Brown proceeded. Early in 1859, he rented a farmhouse near Harpers Ferry and gathered twenty-one men, two of whom were his sons and five of whom were black.

On October 16, Brown and his men attacked the arsenal, which was on a point of land between the Potomac and Shenandoah rivers; shortly afterward, they were cornered by militiamen. The next morning, a small force of U.S. Marines under Robert E. Lee—soon to command Confederate forces in Virginia—forced Brown to surrender. In the raid, most of Brown's men and one innocent onlooker lost their lives. As Brown lay wounded, he was asked, "On what principle do you justify your acts?"

Brown replied quietly, "Upon the Golden Rule. I pity the poor in bondage that have none to help them; that is why I am here; not to gratify any personal animosity, revenge or vindictive spirit. It is my sympathy with the oppressed and wronged, that are as good as you and as precious in the sight of God....You may dispose of me easily but this question is still to be settled—this Negro question—the end of that is still not yet."

In Charles Town, Virginia, Brown was tried and convicted.* On December 2, 1859, he was hanged in Charles Town, in a dusty lot between McCurdy Street and Beckwith Alley. After he was pulled up short by the rope around his neck, one of the fifteen hundred soldiers taking part in the proceeding shouted, "So perisheth all such enemies of Virginia, all such enemies of the Union, all such foes of the human race!"

Not even the most radical of abolitionists, some of whom had given money to Brown's cause, failed to question Brown's methods, but, frustrated by years of talk and little action, many abolitionists thought of him as a saint. Theodore Parker, who had taken part in the attempt to free Anthony Burns, lay dying in a retreat in Italy but found the strength to proclaim, "The road to heaven is as short from the gallows as from a throne."

Poet and philosopher Ralph Waldo Emerson declared that Brown had made "the gallows as glorious as the cross."

Once war began, Union soldiers were to be reminded often of the martyr as they sang their favorite marching song, "John Brown's Body," in which Brown was celebrated as "a soldier in the army of the Lord."

Much as she admired both Garrison and Whittier, Charlotte was no pacifist. It is not surprising, then, that when she visited the Boston Athenaeum, where a marble bust of Brown was on display, she stood silently before the sculpture and paid her respects to him.

---

* *Harpers Ferry and Charles Town are now in West Virginia, which became a separate state in 1863.*

7

"Mr. Lincoln stands hesitating today"

"Salem. June 22, 1862. More penitent than ever I come to thee again old Journal, long neglected friend. More than two years have elapsed since I last talked to thee."

Charlotte summed up her two years of silence. In the fall of 1859 she taught at Higginson; then, in the spring, "had a violent attack of lung fever, which brought me very, very near the grave." She went to Worcester, Massachusetts, for what she called a water cure.

At the Worcester Hydropathic Institution, Charlotte was in the care of a young, attractive doctor named Seth Rogers. Later, quite by chance, they both went to Port Royal—she as a teacher, he as an army surgeon—and, though he was a married man, in the magical southland they were to share a romantic friendship, together taking moonlit horseback rides and attending the exotic gatherings of missionaries, island folk, and soldiers.

Worcester, forty miles west of Boston, was made up of churches, mansions, modest dwellings, schools, and factories, surrounded by the fields of Massachusetts farmers. Most of the cures the Hydropathic Institution offered we now recognize as worthless. Patients were enfolded in wet sheets, advised to eat stale whole wheat bread, take cold showers, confine themselves to cheerful conversations at mealtimes, and sleep with their windows open. They were subjected to electromagnetic treatments, in which mild electric shocks were delivered to the ailing portions of their bodies. Charlotte, believing in these remedies and attracted to her doctor, wrote that "the excellent Dr. Rogers did me a world of good—spiritually as well as physically....In my heart I shall thank him always."

In the spring of 1860 Charlotte took a lively interest in the presidential contest in which Abraham Lincoln ran against three opponents—Stephen Douglas, who had debated Lincoln many times; John Breckenridge; and John Bell. Lincoln won the election and took office on March 15, 1861.

In New Orleans, Lincoln had seen slaves on display and people sold in the same manner as were mules, casks of rum, and bales of cotton. On a riverboat, he had seen slaves in chains. Six years before his first presidential campaign, he had proclaimed that he hated slavery, because it forced good people into "an open war with the very fundamental principles of civil liberty."

Above all, Lincoln was a Unionist, believing that "a house divided against itself cannot stand." He knew that war was coming and he saw the need to compromise, so that the border states and territories wouldn't join the southern states in a conflict with the federal government.

Charlotte admired only the most radical of abolitionists and had little patience with a man who compromised. She thought that the president was weak and indecisive. It was only later that she understood what Massachusetts governor John Andrew had declared after meeting Lincoln at the Republican Convention in Chicago. Andrew had "seen in a flash that here was a man who was master of himself. For the first time, the delegates understood that he whom they had supposed to be little more than a loquacious and clever politician, had force, insight, conscience...."

After teaching briefly, Charlotte once again found herself too weak to go on working and went home to Philadelphia, where she spent the winter. In May 1861 she began another season with the Purvis family, in Bucks County. In view of what we know now about tuberculosis,

Abraham Lincoln, January 15, 1861.

it seems a miracle that she lived past her twenty-first birthday. Prolonged exposure to a tuberculosis victim makes contagion more than likely. Charlotte, probably already suffering from a form of the disease, had nursed Amy Matilda Remond. Now she took care of her cousin Robert Purvis, Jr. "All the beautiful summer I stayed there trying to nurse him and amuse him as well as I could. It was sad to see anyone so young, so full of energy and ambition, doomed to lead a life of inaction....He seemed to improve as the summer advanced and, in the fall, I left him, to take charge of Aunt Margaretta's school in the city—a small school but the children were mostly bright and interesting...."

In the fall of 1861, Henry Cassey, by then a man of twenty, turned up at 92 Lombard Street, having recently returned from France. Cassey's business—probably inherited from his father—kept him in Philadelphia. Charlotte wrote, "He has improved very much and was a very pleasant companion for me all through the winter....He read to me in both French and English....He and I have many things in common and saw much of each other. Of course, people talked and many very sagely said that we were engaged. We heard of it with amusement, for nothing could be more absurd."

In March 1862, Robert Purvis, Jr., died. "When I saw him lying so cold and still, and witnessed the agony of the loving hearts around him, I wished that I could have been taken instead of him. He had everything to live for...."

In May, "Henry went to New York, on his way to Toronto....I missed him sadly, and was not afraid to say so. Let people say what they might. He has a noble nature, and high aspirations, both moral and mental...." These qualities, Charlotte felt, set Henry apart from the vast majority of young men she had met. A year before, she had written, "I *have* a loving heart, though some may doubt it." Few people who knew Charlotte doubted it, and it was clear that she longed for a husband who shared her ideals, her taste in literature, and love of foreign languages, but she was not in love with Henry Cassey and she chose to treat him only as a brother.

Shortly after Henry left, Mary Shephard wrote to Charlotte, asking her to teach summer courses. Once again, Charlotte headed for New England.

In July, almost fifteen months after the beginning of the Civil War, she went with Sarah Cassey to an antislavery meeting in the Boston Music Hall. "The heat was so intense that I could scarcely breathe." She thought of leaving, but as Wendell Phillips started speaking, she "forgot everything else. It was a grand and glorious speech, such as he alone could make."

Wendell Phillips was another abolitionist who refused to consider compromise. He knew and sympathized with Senator Charles Sumner, who had gone on evening drives with Lincoln and had urged him to issue an emancipation proclamation.

Phillips was fifty-one. His sideburns swept down from his ears almost to the corners of his mouth. His lips were thin and he had a downward-curving nose. His voice was magnificent. In his speech, he asked a question. "Mr. Lincoln stands hesitating today. Why? He is 'Honest Abe.' He means to do his duty." Referring to the president and the war, he said, "I believe he honestly wishes this convulsion shall result in the destruction of the slave system."

After hearing Phillips's speech, Charlotte wrote, "I wish the poor miserable President, whom he so justly criticized, could have heard it."

Neither Charlotte nor Phillips could have known that, even as they criticized him, Lincoln was at work on his Emancipation Proclamation. Nor could she have guessed that on January 1, 1863—the day of the issuance of the Emancipation Proclamation—she would be in Port Royal, where she would celebrate Lincoln's action in the company of abolitionists, freed slaves, and soldiers serving in black Union regiments.

John Greenleaf Whittier was responsible for Charlotte's sojourn in South Carolina. On August 9, 1862, she and Mary Shephard went to Amesbury to visit him and his sister. After talking about his escapes from admirers, Whittier "said he was thankful to live in such a quiet little place as Amesbury, where nobody said anything to him about his writings, and where he was not thought of as a writer."

On that day, Whittier urged Charlotte to go south to Port Royal, to teach the children of the contrabands. "Whittier advised me to apply to the Port Royal Commission, in Boston. He is very desirous that I should go. I shall certainly take his advice."

After she encountered a delay in Boston, she returned to Philadelphia to apply to the Port Royal Relief Association there. She was accepted and left New York for Hilton Head on October 22, 1862.

"*They stole away at night*"

During her first few days in Port Royal, while she was living at The Oaks, Charlotte learned the ways of the house servants, who called themselves Swonga people—slaves, certainly, but a proud and privileged class. The Swonga women had spent their lives serving their white mistresses and masters and were willing to take care of the white people who proposed to educate their children and themselves, but at first they were reluctant to do anything for Charlotte. Laura Towne, in charge of educating the children of the contrabands, remembered, "Aunt Becky required some coaxing to wait on her and do her room."

Schoolteachers' house in Beaufort, South Carolina.

Union ships bombarding the defenses at Port Royal, November 1861.

Soon Charlotte's natural dignity and her sympathetic nature began to change Aunt Becky's mind. A friend remembered that the question was resolved when they heard Charlotte play the piano. After that everyone admired her and grew fond of her.

Laura Towne told Charlotte about the occupation of the islands. On November 7, 1861, referred to by the contrabands as the "day of the big gun shoot," a fleet of Union warships under the command of Commodore S. F. Du Pont had sailed across Port Royal Sound and opened fire on Confederate forts and gun emplacements, reducing them to rubble. South Carolinian James Pettigrew, who loved his native state but was loyal to the Union, remarked, "On the islands a discovery is made which the inhabitants were slow in coming to, that in a war with an enemy that is master of the sea they are masters of nothing."

Some planters had escaped to the mainland before Du Pont's flotilla entered Port Royal Sound, but few had believed that their enemy would occupy a region that produced so valuable a crop as

Laura Towne and three of her students.

cotton. Most left at the last minute, abandoning their field hands and all but a few of their house servants.

Eight months before Charlotte arrived at Hilton Head, Edward Pierce, a young Boston lawyer, had brought sixty antislavery missionaries, fifteen of whom were women, to the islands. Later, when Charlotte met him, she found Pierce "entertaining. There's something in his manner—such a graceful geniality—that makes it very easy to talk with him...." Pierce grew fond of her and presented her with a pearl-handled knife that had been given him by Charles Sumner.

Pierce's purpose was to educate the contrabands—teach them to read and write, help them raise the food they needed to survive, teach them a little medicine, and urge them to grow cotton to be sold to textile factories in the North. This enterprise, called the Port Royal

Experiment, was to be a first step in the rehabilitation of the South.

Pierce found himself constantly in conflict with Northern profiteers. The planters had told their slaves that, if they stayed behind, the Yankees would imprison them and sell them into slavery. Few, if any, had believed their masters, but, as it happened, one unscrupulous New Englander—not one of Pierce's people—was discovered as he was about to sell a shipload of contrabands to a Cuban slave dealer. This offense was not repeated, but as often as they could, Yankee cotton brokers cheated Pierce.

Charlotte and the Hunns lived at The Oaks a week or so, then moved to Oaklands, a much smaller and less comfortable plantation house that was closer to the red brick Baptist church where Charlotte taught. The house was a single-story wood frame building with a porch across its front. Its interior had been scrubbed and whitewashed, but the place had been stripped of most of its furniture. "Mr. Hunn had not had time to get the mattresses, in New York, so I suppose we must use blanket substitutes...," Charlotte wrote. "I am determined not to be discouraged at anything. I have never felt more hopeful, more cheerful than I do now."

Two days later she wrote, "Our home looks rather desolate; the only furniture consisting of two bureaus, three small pine tables and two chairs, one of which has a broken back. Lizzie and I have manufactured a small rug of some woolen stuff, red and black plaid, which will give our parlor a somewhat more comfortable look." Charlotte had brought with her an engraving for *Evangeline*, Henry Wadsworth Longfellow's epic poem. "I have already hung up my Evangeline, and two or three other prints, and gathered some beautiful roses."

Mr. Hunn set up his store in the house and Lizzie helped her father organize its offerings, while Charlotte walked alone to school "through lovely woods just brightening to scarlet now."

Her first full day of teaching was "not a very pleasant one. Some of my scholars are very tiny—babies I call them—and it is hard to keep them quiet and interested while I am hearing the larger ones. They are too young even for the alphabet, it seems to me. I think I must write home and ask somebody to send me picture books and toys to amuse them with."

At the school she worked with teacher Ellen Murray, a young woman with blue eyes and corkscrew curls. Charlotte wrote, "She is very loveable."

Charlotte learned to occupy the little ones while she taught the older students history. She told them about John Brown and about the magnificent Toussaint L'Ouverture, the Haitian revolutionary who had learned to perform surgery and had served as a physician to his people. In 1791 Toussaint joined in a revolt against French rule, serving first as a surgeon, then as a military strategist and commander. When his powerful black army triumphed in the field, Toussaint declared himself the ruler of the island. Though the French had freed their slaves in 1793, they wanted to continue to rule Haiti, and Toussaint was captured, sent to France, and imprisoned. He died in jail.

The people of St. Helena and the surrounding islands spoke mostly Gullah—a melodic dialect that had come from Africa—but they recognized the importance of the English language and the power of the written word. Adults as well as children wanted to be taught how to read and write. "This evening, Harry—one of the men on the place—came in for a lesson. He is most eager to learn and is a scholar to be proud of....He held his pen almost perfectly right the first time. He will very soon learn to write, I think." Harry's progress prompted Charlotte to round up other people "who would like to take lessons at night."

Charlotte's favorite contraband was a handyman named Cupid, a name she said was common in the islands. She described him as "a

Schoolteacher Ellen Murray and students.

small wry figure, stockingless, shoeless, out at the knees and elbows, and wearing the remnant of an old straw hat, which looked as if it might have done good service in scaring the crows from a cornfield." Cupid's face was "nearly black, very ugly, but with the shrewdest expression I ever saw, and the brightest, most humorous twinkle in the eyes. One glance at Cupid's face showed that he was not a person to be imposed upon, and that he was abundantly able to take care of himself, as well as of us."

Sometimes at night, the children came to Oaklands to entertain Charlotte, the Hunns, and Cupid with a shout—much like a ritual that was performed in Africa. "The children form a ring and move around in a kind of shuffling dance, singing all the time. Four or five stand apart and sing very energetically, clapping their hands, stamping their feet and rocking their bodies to and fro."

Because Charlotte took an interest in them, the field hands talked to her about their lives as slaves and their escapes from slavery. An island woman named Tina told her an inspiring story. Two girls, one ten and the other fifteen, "who having been taken by their master up into the country about the time of the 'big gun shoot,' determined to try to get back to their parents who had been left on this island. They stole away at night and traveled through woods and swamps, for two days without eating. Sometimes their strength would fail and they would sink down in the swamps, and think they could go no further, but they had brave little hearts and struggled on, until at last they reached Port Royal ferry. There they were seen by a boatload of people who had also made their escape. The boat was too full to take them but the people, as soon as they reached these islands, told the father of the children, who immediately hastened to the ferry for them. The poor little creatures were almost wild with joy, despite their exhausted state, when they saw their father coming to them. When they were brought to their mother, she fell down 'just as if she was dead' as Tina expressed it, she was so overpowered with joy."

Some planters had the welfare of their slaves in mind. John Fripp, a sour-looking man who was a Union sympathizer, turned out to be one of these. He called his slaves together and told them that on the mainland they might starve. He suggested that they hide until the Union soldiers landed, then forget about the cotton crop and work together to raise food for themselves and their children.

Charlotte chose to believe that it was Union soldiers who had sacked the houses of the planters—taking furniture, works of art, and other valuables—and that the slaves had taken only what was left. In fact, because Commodore Du Pont was slow to land the soldiers, it was the slaves who had first pickings. Some took things for their own use, but others, angry and frustrated after years of servitude, smashed things treasured by their masters and destroyed the organs in two churches.

Most slaves chose to escape and most masters let them go, but some of the overseers who had spent their lives subduing black men—driving them like beasts of burden, cursing them, and whipping them—couldn't stand being disobeyed. A contraband named Will told Charlotte that he knew of thirty black men who had been killed for refusing to go with their masters to the mainland.

Charlotte was attracted to a child who came often to Oaklands. "I am quite in love with one of the children here—little Amaretta, who is niece to our good old Amaretta. She is a cunning little kittenish thing with such a demure look." Always aware of color, Charlotte added, "She is not quite black, and has pretty, close hair and delicate features. She is bright too. I love the child. Wish I could take her for my own."

Charlotte wrote of a young mother, Tillah. "Poor creature, she has a dear little baby, Annie, who for weeks has been dangerously ill with whooping cough and fever." Laura Towne, who had a bag of medicines, made the rounds of the slave quarters and took care of the sick

Former Sea Island slaves harvesting sweet potatoes, 1863.

people, using simple remedies. Charlotte often went with her and had grown fond of Tillah.

Ten days later, Charlotte wrote, "Came home, and soon afterward, to my great grief, heard that Tillah's dear little baby was dead. It was really a shock to me....I hastened at once to the cabin." The child was lying in her grandmother's lap "looking as if it were sleeping sweetly. The poor mother sat by looking so very sad. My heart aches for her. During eight weeks she has been constantly devoted to the child—her only little girl—and we hoped she would be rewarded by having it spared to her....It was one of the loveliest, most interesting babies I ever saw."

Two weeks after Tillah's baby died, Charlotte wrote, "Christmas Day, 1862. A bright and lovely Christmas day. We were waked early by the people knocking at our window and shouting 'Merry Christmas.' After breakfast, we went out and distributed the presents—to each of the babies a bright red dress, and little Jessie a white apron trimmed with crochet braid, and to each of the other children an apron and an orange. To each of the workers a pie—an apple pie—which pleased them very much."

At the church, the teachers led the people in the singing of songs and hymns. One of the hymns had been contributed by Whittier. Charlotte noted, "A few days before Christmas, we were delighted at receiving a beautiful Christmas Hymn from Whittier, written by request, especially for our children. They learned it very easily and enjoyed singing it. We showed them the writer's picture, and told them he was a very good friend of theirs...."

The people had "several grand shouts, in the entry. 'Look upon the Lord,' which they sang tonight, seems to me the most beautiful of all their shouting tunes. There is something in it that goes to the depths of one's soul." That night Charlotte went to bed tired but happy, looking forward to another celebration, six days hence.

CHAPTER

9

"I hail it as the doom of slavery"

On the day of the issuance of the Emancipation Proclamation, Charlotte wrote, "Thursday, New Year's Day, 1863. The most glorious day this nation has yet seen...."

Abolitionists had long urged the president to free the slaves, *all* the slaves in *all* the states and territories, but for two years Lincoln had been waiting for a Union victory in the East. The Battle of Antietam, fought in Sharpsburg, Maryland, on September 17, 1862, was seen by Lincoln as a turning point, if not a victory. Following the war's most costly single day of fighting, the Army of Northern Virginia, under General Robert E. Lee, had been forced to retire—although it had not been pursued and destroyed by the much stronger Union forces under General George B. McClellan. Unsatisfactory as the outcome of the battle had been, Lincoln knew that, at last, the time had come to make his intentions known.

He had begun to shape the Emancipation Proclamation in the spring of 1862. Almost every day he went to the War Department to read dispatches from his generals, and it was there, in the telegraph office, that he began to write the proclamation.

Thomas Eckert, who was in charge of the office, didn't know until later what the president was working on. At first Lincoln, sitting at a borrowed desk, wrote only a few words. Eckert remembered that he stared for minutes at a time at a family of large spiders who had been allowed to spin a web above the desk.

Lincoln read a draft to the members of his cabinet in July, and on

September 22, five days after Antietam, he presented to them what he called a preliminary proclamation, promising that emancipation would become effective on January 1, 1863.

In its first paragraph the final proclamation stated, "That on the 1st day of January, A.D. 1863, all persons held as slaves within any State or designated part of a State the people whereof shall then be in rebellion against the United States shall be then, thenceforward, and forever free...."

Frederick Douglass saw at once that the proclamation changed the purpose of the war. He said, "I hail it as the doom of slavery in all the States."

In Confederate territory occupied by the Union—in South Carolina and Louisiana—and in Kansas, Union regiments whose enlisted men were black had been organized with no more than a halfhearted nod from the federal government. The Confederate government, fearing slave uprisings, hadn't dared arm its slaves but had used thousands of them in support of its armies, as servants, laborers, and teamsters. Black men were already serving in the Union navy, and now, with issuance of his Emancipation Proclamation, the president was welcoming thousands of free black men into military service. "And I further declare and make it known that such persons of suitable condition will be received into the armed services of the United States to garrison forts, positions, stations, and other places, and to man vessels of all sorts in said service." In short, Lincoln's proclamation made it possible for large numbers of black men to go to war to free their brothers in the South and to gain equality and justice for themselves. Before the war came to an end, more than 200,000 black men were to serve the Union in the army and the navy.

On New Year's morning, Charlotte went to Beaufort, where she went aboard the riverboat *Flora*, which was bound for Camp Saxton, headquarters of the First Regiment of South Carolina Volunteers under the command of Colonel Thomas Wentworth Higginson. Higginson had been among those abolitionists who tried to rescue fugitive slave Anthony Burns from the Boston jail in 1854. As the *Flora* made its way across the sunlit waters, Charlotte noted that it carried "an eager, wondering crowd of the freed people in their holiday attire—the gayest of head-handkerchiefs, the whitest of aprons.... The band was playing, the flags streaming, everybody talking merrily...."

Charlotte wrote, "Just as my foot touched the plank, on landing, a hand grasped mine and a well known voice spoke my name. It was my dear friend Dr. Seth Rogers." She added, "How delighted I was to see him; how *good* it was to see the face of a friend from the North, and *such* a friend." Then "walking on a little distance I found myself being presented to Colonel Higginson. I was so much overwhelmed that I had no reply to make to the very kind and courteous little speech with which he met me. I believe I mumbled something...."

Charlotte sat on the reviewing stand. "There were the black soldiers, in their blue coats and scarlet pants, and the officers of this and other regiments in their handsome uniforms, and some crowds of onlookers, men, women and children, grouped in various attitudes, under the trees. Their faces wore a happy, eager, expectant look...."

A local minister read the entire Emancipation Proclamation and Chaplain Mansfield French, serving with Higginson, gave a speech about its meaning. Charlotte wrote that, when French finished speaking, "some of the colored people—of their own accord—sang 'My Country 'Tis of Thee.' It was a touching and beautiful incident and Colonel Higginson made it the occasion of some happy remarks. He said that *that* tribute was far more affecting than any speech he could make. Nothing could have been better, more perfect. And Dr. Rogers told me afterward

Edward Pierce talks to a group of former slaves.

that the Colonel was much affected, that tears were in his eyes."

Robert Sutton, a handsome black noncommissioned officer who was soon to become a hero, made a touching and impressive speech, and General Rufus Saxton, Beaufort's military governor, topped off the ceremonies, praising both the proclamation and the troops in his command. After lunch the First South Carolina marched for the assembled company. "The dress parade—the first I have ever seen—delighted me. It was a brilliant sight—the long line of men in their bright uniforms, with bayonets gleaming in the sunlight."

Meanwhile, on St. Helena, the missionaries faced a growing problem. Nearby Edisto Island, no longer occupied by Union troops, wasn't safe from enemy attacks, and refugees from Edisto and other smaller islands came to St. Helena. One chilly Saturday, Charlotte and Lizzie Hunn took a buggy ride to a neighboring plantation. Charlotte wrote that two supervisors "took us around to see the people, of whom there are 150 on the place. 100 have come from Edisto. There were no houses to accommodate so many and they had to find shelter in barns and outbuildings....They have constructed rude houses for themselves—many of which do not, however, afford them much protection in bad weather. I am told that they are all excellent industrious people.

"One old woman interested me deeply. Her name is Daphne, and she is probably at least 100 years old. She has had 50 grandchildren, 65 great-grandchildren, and three great-great-grandchildren. She is entirely blind but seems quite cheerful and happy. She told us that she was brought from Africa to this country just after the Revolution."

Most slaves were called by given names and had no family names. Some of these chose family names for themselves and asked that they be baptized. Charlotte wrote, "Saw a wonderful sight today. 150 people were baptized in the creek near the church. They looked very picturesque—many of them in white aprons." As they marched down to the water in a long procession "they sang beautifully."

Many men and women who had lived as slaves, and had accordingly been denied the right to marry, were joined in wedlock in impressive ceremonies.

On January 31, Charlotte visited Harriet Tubman, hero of the Underground Railroad. Tubman, then in her early forties, was a brilliant woman, small and fiercely energetic. She had escaped from slavery in 1849, had known John Brown, and was admired and trusted by many other leading abolitionists. Having been a field hand, she was tough and absolutely fearless. When Charlotte met her, she was acting as a scout for the Union. Charlotte wrote, "She is a wonderful woman....She told me that she used to hide people in the woods, during the day, and go around and get provisions for them. Once, she had with her a man named Joe, for whom a reward of $1,500 was offered. Frequently, in different places, she found handbills exactly describing him." At last, they reached Canada. "Until then, Joe had been very silent. In vain had she called his attention to the glory of a waterfall. He sat perfectly still—moody it seemed—and would not even glance at them but when she said, 'Now we are in Canada,' he sprang to his feet, with a great shout,

Harriet Tubman.

and sang and clapped his hands in a perfect delirium of joy."

Toward the end of January, Higginson's regiment made a raid on the mainland, steaming up the St. Marys River, between Florida and Georgia. When the regiment returned, Rogers came to visit Charlotte. "Dr. Rogers described beautifully the scenes through which they passed, particularly the night journey up the river, with the good old oaks on either side."

In his first fight, Corporal Robert Sutton proved his mettle. Charlotte noted, "The noble Robert Sutton, whom Colonel Higginson called 'the leader of the expedition,' was wounded in three places and still kept to his post."

Higginson reported, "Nobody knows anything about these men who has not seen them in battle. I find that I myself knew nothing. There is a fiery energy about them...."

The regiment raided a plantation where the widow of its owner lived alone. The woman said that she and her husband had been kind to their slaves, but Corporal Sutton, who had been one of them, "said the people were cruelly treated, and the jail on the place, where chains and handcuffs were found, bears witness to that. The soldiers brought off cattle, horses and lumber...."

Seth Rogers saw as much of Charlotte as he could. At first, in Worcester, she had depended on him and had grown fond of him. In the islands, he developed an affection for her. His attentions made her happy. "The kind and loving words he spoke to me tonight sank deep into my heart." She was pleased when he asked her to consider him a brother and responded, "I will gladly do so."

Devoted as she was to Rogers, she seemed always in control of her emotions and expressed amusement at a couple who displayed their affection for each other openly. One evening, at a party, she observed that her fellow teacher Ellen Murray was in love with Mansfield French, Jr., son of Chaplain Mansfield French, and he with her. Charlotte remarked, "Ah love! 'Tis a queer thing, but very amusing to lookers-on."

One day, after a long absence, Rogers stopped at the school to visit Charlotte. She exulted, "Wasn't I glad to see him! Miss Murray *would* have the children read to him, and they read remarkably well. He praised them. They sang beautifully too, which delighted him. He came home to dine with us, and then we—just he and I—had the loveliest horseback ride to Mr. Thorpe's place." They rode through the pines and "found the most exquisite jessamine....Nothing could be more perfect than the color, more delicious than the fragrance. Dr. Rogers broke off long sprays and twined them around me. I felt grand as a queen."

Mr. Thorpe was not at home so they turned back. Charlotte wrote as if addressing a close friend. "I can give you no idea of the ride homeward. I know only that it was the most delightful ride I ever had in my life. The young moon—just a silver bow—had the most singular, almost violet tinge, and all around it in the heavens was a rosy glow, deepening every moment...."

10

"The morning star is bright upon the horizon!"

In March, Charlotte heard about the Fifty-fourth Massachusetts Volunteers, the first black regiment organized after Lincoln's issuance of the Emancipation Proclamation. She heard that its young officers were the sons of dedicated abolitionists, that its ranks were being filled with free men of the highest character. She never guessed that the regiment would come south to Port Royal and establish its headquarters at Land's End, on St. Helena, six miles from where she lived.

Governor John Andrew was the father of the regiment. In early January he had gone to Washington and obtained an order giving him permission to send out officers and agents to recruit in Massachusetts. He would have liked to appoint black officers, but he knew that he would first have to concentrate on campaigning for the rights of his enlisted men—to receive equal pay, to bear arms, to engage in major battles—before he could insist that the best of them become commissioned officers.

Andrew soon extended his recruiting efforts to include other states and Canada. Frederick Douglass went to work in New York State. The great black leader's first recruit was his son Lewis, who became sergeant major of the regiment. In Rochester, Douglass spoke to a group of young black men. "A war undertaken and brazenly carried on for the perpetual enslavement of colored men calls logically and loudly upon colored men to help suppress it." He went on: "I will not argue. To do so implies hesitation and doubt, and you do not hesitate.

You do not doubt. The day dawns—the morning star is bright upon the horizon! The iron gate of our prison stands half open. One gallant rush from the North will fling it wide open, while four millions of our brothers and sisters shall march out into Liberty!"

In February, Robert Gould Shaw took command of the pioneering regiment. He was short, blond, and blue-eyed. In his childhood and his youth he had been pampered by rich parents, both of whom were abolitionists. In his youth he lived in Europe—first at a school in Switzerland, then in Italy and Germany. Back in America, he went to Harvard University but dropped out in his junior year to go to work for an uncle in New York. As the Civil War began, he joined the Seventh New York National Guard and, as a private, went to the defense of Washington. With a friend he paid a call on Lincoln and

A Union army camp in the Sea Islands.

Henry Stewart, a soldier in the Fifty-fourth Massachusetts Volunteers.

observed, "It is really too bad to call him one of the ugliest men in the country, for I have seldom seen a pleasanter or more kind-hearted one, and he has certainly a very striking face."

A month later, Shaw left the Seventh and became an officer in the Second Massachusetts Infantry, a regiment in which many officers were, like him, young men from privileged families. Though he missed his parents and four sisters, he fought bravely and was praised by his men for his coolness under fire.

On January 30, Andrew asked Shaw to command the Fifty-fourth. Shaw refused. He found it hard to think of leaving comrades in the Second. A friend of his who understood his hesitation said later, "In this new negro-soldier venture, loneliness was certain, ridicule inevitable, failure possible; and Shaw was only 25; and although he had stood among the bullets at Cedar Mountain and Antietam, he had until then been walking socially on the sunny side of life."

Shaw's father, a gentle, dedicated scholar, understood his son's determination to remain in the Second, but his mother, an intense, crusading woman, wrote to Andrew, "This decision has caused me the bitterest disappointment I have ever experienced." She went on to say that had her son accepted the commission, "it would have been the proudest moment of my life and I could have died satisfied that I had not lived in vain. This being the truth, you will believe that I have shed bitter tears over his refusal."

Shaw wrote to his fiancée, Anna Haggerty, for advice and, finding her supportive, was inclined to change his mind. At last, on February 5, feeling that his refusal had been cowardly, he accepted Andrew's offer. He and Anna married on May 2, and she continued to encourage him, even though she understood that not only would he risk his life in battle but that officers commanding black men might be hanged if they were captured.

By the time Charlotte met him, Shaw was dedicated to his regiment. Not long before, he had written, "Truly I ought to be thankful for all my happiness and success so far; and if the raising of colored troops proves such a benefit to the country and to the blacks, as many people think it will, I shall thank God a thousand times that I was led to take my share in it." After several months of training them, Shaw believed that his men were as good as any soldiers in the Union army. For that reason and because he was a seasoned officer who disliked

Robert Gould Shaw.

guerrilla warfare, he was sickened by his first assignment in the South.

On June 11, Colonel James Montgomery, a thin, soft-spoken man described by Shaw as having a "queer roll or glare in his eye," ordered a company of Shaw's men to join his regiment of contra-bands, the Second South Carolina Volunteers, in burning Darien, a defenseless Georgia town on the Altamaha River. Shaw, who protest-ed but was overruled, believed that the action was a stain on the record of a regiment organized to demonstrate that black Americans could serve bravely and with honor. After the raid, Shaw hoped for a chance to redeem the honor of his regiment, to wipe out the memory of what he called "the Darien affair."

Charlotte met Shaw for the first time on July 2, when he and his second-in-command, Lieutenant Colonel Edward N. Hallowell, were invited to Seaside, the summer quarters that Charlotte shared with several other teachers. Seaside had "a delightful piazza which can be enclosed with blinds, at will." It was there that tea was served to the young officers. Shaw was almost exactly Charlotte's age—just two months younger. She wrote, "I am perfectly charmed with Colonel Shaw. He seems to me one of the most delightful people I have ever met." She added, "I have seen him but once, yet I cannot help feeling a really affectionate admiration for him." After tea, Hallowell went back to Land's End and Shaw stayed awhile at Seaside. Charlotte wrote, "We had a very pleasant talk on the moonlit piazza...."

Shaw praised Charlotte in a letter to his parents. "She is quite pretty, remarkably well educated, and a very interesting woman. She is decidedly the belle here, and the officers of both the army and the navy seem to think her society far preferable to that of the other ladies."

That night Shaw went with Charlotte to what the people called a "Praise House." Shaw remembered, "The praying was done by an old blind fellow, who made believe, all the time, that he was reading out of a book. He was also the leader of the singing, and seemed to throw his whole soul into it."

Charlotte was acquainted with the man who did the praying, and she knew that his blindness had been caused by a blow on the temple with a loaded bullwhip wielded by a master or an overseer. She commented, "Old Maurice surpassed himself tonight, singing 'The tallest tree in Paradise.'"

After the meeting, Shaw and Charlotte watched a shout. Charlotte saw that her companion "looked and listened with the deepest interest and expressed himself much gratified."

July 4 dawned bright and clear. Charlotte drove to the grounds of the red brick Baptist church, where she met Shaw, who wrote later, "The day was beautiful and the crowd was collected in the church-yard under some magnificent old oaks....The gay dresses and turbans of the women made the sight very brilliant.

"Can you imagine anything more wonderful than a colored aboli-tionist meeting on a South Carolina plantation? Here were collected all the freed slaves on this island listening to the most ultra abolition-ist speeches that could be made; while two years ago their masters were still here, the lords of the soil and of them." He commented, "Such things oblige a man to believe that God isn't very far off.

"A little black boy read the Declaration of Independence, and then they all sang some of the hymns. The effect was grand." He added, "Miss Forten promised to write me out the words of some of the hymns they sang, which I will send to you."

Two days later, with three other women, Charlotte rode to the Fifty-fourth's encampment at Land's End. The camp consisted of sev-eral hundred canvas tents bleached white by the summer sun, ranks of wagons, strings of horses—all dwarfed by towering palmetto trees. There, now and then, the voice of a corporal or a sergeant rose above the constant hum of talk, the jingle of harnesses, and the thud of rest-less hooves on the hard-packed sandy soil.

Shaw and Hallowell rode out to meet their guests and led them to a cluster of headquarters tents, which were fronted by a small hastily constructed grandstand on the edge of a parade ground.

"We were just in time to see the dress parade," Charlotte wrote. "'Tis a splendid looking regiment, an honor to the race. Then we went with Colonel Shaw to tea. Afterward, we sat outside his tent and lis-tened to some very fine singing from some of the privates. I am more than ever charmed with Colonel Shaw. What purity, what nobleness of soul, what exquisite gentleness in that beautiful face! As I look at it,

Seaside, Charlotte's summer quarters.

I think 'The bravest are the tenderest.'" She added, "I do think he is a wonderfully loveable person."

Alone, they talked to each other once again and then joined in general conversation. At last the visit ended. "Tonight, he helped me on my horse and, after carefully arranging the folds of my riding skirt, said so kindly, 'Goodbye. If I don't see you again down here I hope to see you at our house.'"

Shaw had requested that the Fifty-fourth be included in a force that was, even then, moving toward its enemy. Two days later, Shaw, Hallowell, and most of the other soldiers of the Fifty-fourth—those not sick or left behind to guard the camp—would be heading northeast to join a variety of other regiments, most of them white, to attack outposts on the islands south of Charleston.

11

"I do give Him the glory"

On July 8, Charlotte drove to Land's End with a Union officer to pick up a soldier who was sick. They found the encampment quiet. "The regiment has gone. Left this morning. My heart-felt prayers go with them—for the men and their noble, noble young Colonel Shaw. God bless him! God keep him in His care!"

Charlotte heard news of important battles, in the East and in the West. On July 1, the greatest battle of the Civil War had begun at Gettysburg—a three-day struggle that had caused Confederate forces to withdraw from Pennsylvania and recross the Potomac, never to return again—and a long and arduous campaign against Vicksburg, Mississippi, had ended in a siege, followed by the surrender of its garrison on July 4.

Union generals in South Carolina, having had enough of token raids on the mainland in which they had failed even to tear up a railroad line, were determined to recapture Fort Sumter, which, more than any other Southern stronghold, was a symbol of rebellion. Its recapture would not only tighten the blockade but would be seen as yet another signal of the coming victory.

To subdue Fort Sumter, they had first to control Morris Island, whose beaches faced the sea and whose slim northern neck reached out toward Fort Sumter. This neck, protected by an earthwork called Fort Wagner, was the only part of Morris Island that remained in the hands of the defenders.

By the time he headed toward the islands south of Charleston,

Shaw was a determined man. Following a fierce hand-to-hand engagement with Confederate soldiers on James Island—next to Morris Island—in which the Fifty-fourth saved a white New England regiment from annihilation, Shaw and his men marched all night through salt marshes in a crashing thunderstorm. On July 17, at dawn, they arrived exhausted at an inlet, where they dozed in the hot sun before they boarded the small steamer that would take them to the southern end of Morris Island. There Shaw wrote his wife. "We have had nothing but crackers and coffee these two days. It seems like old times in the army of the Potomac."

On the steamer he told Hallowell, "Oh Ned! If I could live a few weeks longer…and be home a little while I think I might die happy. But it cannot be. I do not believe I will live through our next fight."

Sitting on the beach at Morris Island looking out across the broad Atlantic, Sergeant Robert Simmons, one of Shaw's finest soldiers, thought back to the engagement on James Island, in which several of his comrades had been lost. He fished in his pack, took out a pad and pencil, and wrote to his mother in New York, "We just fought a desperate battle….God has protected me through this, my first leaden trial, and I do give Him the glory, and render praises unto His holy name." He finished with the words, "God bless you all! Goodbye! Likely we shall be engaged soon. Your affectionate son, R. J. Simmons."

On Morris Island, Shaw received the welcome news that the Fifty-fourth had been transferred to a brigade commanded by George C. Strong, a youthful general he admired, and that Strong might be willing to give Shaw and his men a chance to prove themselves.

News traveled slowly in the islands. Later, Charlotte was to learn what had happened at Fort Wagner. On July 11, while the Fifty-fourth was fighting on James Island, a brigade made up entirely of white soldiers had launched the first attack on the earthwork. The assault was a

Fort Wagner on the morning after the July 18, 1863, assault.

failure, but General Truman Seymour, in command on Morris Island, was determined to attack the fort again. He believed that the continuous bombardment had destroyed Fort Wagner's guns and killed many of its soldiers. In fact, both men and guns had been under cover. Not a single cannon had been damaged or a single soldier killed.

On the afternoon of July 18, Shaw and Hallowell, accompanied by the boom of their own cannon and the cries of sea birds at the water's edge, rode ahead to speak to Strong, and Strong, knowing of their eagerness to take part in the attack, looked Shaw in the eye and said, "You may lead the column if you say yes. Your men, I know, are worn out, but do as you choose." Shaw brightened and told Hallowell to bring up the regiment.

Edward Pierce had come to Morris Island to observe the assault and to report on it. Shaw spoke to Pierce, asking him to take note of the bravery of his men on James Island.

That evening, as a mist settled on the depths of the Atlantic, Shaw dismounted, sent his horse to the rear, and walked among his soldiers, speaking softly, demonstrating his affection for them. Without dishonoring himself, Shaw could have marched behind his flag bearers, but he signaled his intention to go first, and in response his men sent up a rousing cheer.

As the Fifty-fourth advanced, both attacking and defending guns were silent. No sound issued from the battered pile of palmetto logs, earth, and sand that comprised Fort Wagner. The pounding sea was close to Shaw, on his right. A salt marsh lay on his left. As the path grew narrower, Shaw walked faster, peering into growing darkness. Behind him, the Stars and Stripes and the Massachusetts flag rippled, fell, and rose again in the night wind.

The ranks grew ragged as the path narrowed further. The shrill voice of a Confederate officer pierced the silence and was followed by a storm of rifle fire. An attacking officer remembered, "A sheet of flame, followed by a running fire, like electric sparks, swept along the parapet."

Shaw started running toward the fort. A moat lay in front of him, at the base of the earthwork—a ditch fed by the rising waters of the sea. His flag bearers and his leading officers and men followed him as he waded through the waist-high waters, scrambled upward, clawing at the sloping wall of sand. At last he reached the parapet. A silhouette against the smoke and flame, his sword pointing toward the sky, he shouted to his men to follow him.

On July 20 Charlotte wrote, "For nearly two weeks we have waited, oh how anxiously, for news of our regiment which went, we know, to Morris Island, to take part in the attack on Charleston. Tonight comes news, oh so sad, so heart sickening. It is too terrible, too terrible to write. We can only hope that it may not all be true—that our noble, beautiful young

Colonel Shaw is killed and the regiment cut to pieces! I cannot, cannot believe it. And yet I know it may be so. But, oh, I am stunned, sick at heart. I can scarcely write. There was an attack on Fort Wagner. The Fifty-fourth, put in advance, fought bravely, desperately, but was finally over-powered and driven back after getting into the fort. Thank Heaven! They fought bravely! And, oh, I must hope that our colonel, *ours* especially he seems to me, is not killed. But I can write no more tonight."

12

"God grant that he may indeed be living"

On Tuesday, July 21, Charlotte heard that wounded soldiers of the Fifty-fourth had been brought from Morris Island to Port Royal for treatment, that hospitals on the Beaufort waterfront were overburdened. She asked Ellen Murray to teach classes for her, packed some things, and went to the Port Royal ferry. "Came down today, hearing that nurses were badly needed."

She went first to her quarters, a room on the second floor of a tall house occupied by nurses and schoolteachers, then to "a large brick building, quite close to the water, two-storied, has many windows and is very airy—in every way adapted to a hospital."

While she waited to start nursing, General Rufus Saxton's wife asked her to mend uniforms. "It was with a full heart that I sewed up bullet holes and bayonet cuts. Sometimes I found a jacket that told a sad tale—so torn to pieces that it was far past mending.

"After awhile, I went through the wards. As I passed along I thought, 'Many and low are the pallets, but each is the face of a friend.' And I was surprised to see such cheerful faces looking up from the beds."

At first, she did simple chores—giving out medicines and helping to change bandages. Late that evening she returned to her quarters and took time to bring her journal up to date.

At dawn she walked through Beaufort's silent streets to return to the hospital, where the lamps had burned all night. Most of the soldiers of the Fifty-fourth, having been craftsmen or professionals, knew how to read and write, but their wounds kept some of them from writing home. "I was employed part of the time in writing letters for the men....Talked with them much today."

She relayed a rumor to Shaw's wounded soldiers. "Told them that we had heard that their noble colonel was not dead, but had been taken prisoner....How joyfully their wan faces lighted up! They almost started from their couches....Their attachment to their gallant young colonel is beautiful to see. How warmly, how enthusiastically they speak of him. 'He was one of the best in the world,' they said. 'No one could be kinder to a set of men than he was to us.' Brave hearts! I hope they will ever prove worthy of such a leader. God grant that he may indeed be living. But I fear, I greatly fear it may be a false report."

Praying that Shaw might be alive, Charlotte gave her full attention to his soldiers. "One fellow here interests me greatly. He is very young, only nineteen, and comes from Michigan. He is badly wounded in both legs and there is a ball in his stomach—it is thought that cannot be extracted. This poor fellow suffers terribly. His groans are pitiful to hear. But he utters no complaint, and it is touching to see his gratitude for the least kindnesses that one does him." She added, "He is an only son and had come away against his mother's will. He would not have her written to until he was better. Poor fellow! That will never be, in this world." Later, Charlotte was surprised to hear that the young man had recovered.

"Another, a sergeant, suffers great pain, being badly wounded in the leg. But he too lies perfectly patient and uncomplaining. He has such a good, honest face....He is said to be one of the bravest and best men in the regiment.

"Brave fellows! I feel it a happiness, an honor, to do the slightest service for them. True, they were unsuccessful in the attack on Fort Wagner but that was no fault of theirs. It is the testimony of all that they fought bravely as men can fight, and that it was only when completely overwhelmed by superior numbers that they were driven back."

On Friday, July 24, six days after the attack on Wagner, Charlotte wrote, "Today the news of Colonel Shaw's death is confirmed. There can no longer be any doubt. It makes me sad, sad at heart. They say he sprang from the parapet of the fort and cried, 'Onward, my brave boys, onward,' then fell, pierced with wounds. I know it was a glorious death. But oh, it is hard, very hard for the young wife, so late a bride, for the mother, whose only and most dearly loved son he was—that heroic mother who rejoiced in the position which he occupied as colonel of a colored regiment.

"I recall him as a much loved friend. Yet I saw him but a few times....Oh it is terrible. It seems very, very hard to me that the best and noblest must be the earliest called away. Especially has it been throughout this dreadful war."

Edward Pierce, back from Morris Island, went with Charlotte to the officers' hospital. There she saw Colonel Hallowell "who, though badly wounded in three places, is improving.

"With deep sadness he spoke of Colonel Shaw and then told me something that greatly surprised me—that the colonel, before that fatal attack, had told him that in case he fell he wished me to have one of his horses—he had three very fine spirited ones that he had brought from the North. How very, very kind it was! I shall treasure this gift sacredly all my life long."

On Sunday, Charlotte rested. Exhausted, she wrote, "Have become so weak that I fear I should be easy prey to the fever which prevails here, a little later in the season."

She had a talk with Seth Rogers, after which she came "to the very sudden determination to go north in the next steamer."

Five days later, with Rogers, Pierce, and other people she had known in the islands, she sailed aboard the steamship *Fulton* to New York. "The waves are a rich deep green, the sky a lovely blue, the sun shines brightly. It is very, very pleasant at sea.

"Early this afternoon, we came in sight of Charleston....Had an excellent view of Fort Sumter, which seems to rise out of the water—bold, grim and most formidable looking. In the distance, we could see the smoke from the guns on Morris Island and, through a glass, caught a very indistinct view of Fort Wagner. I shudder at the thought of that place, remembering the beautiful and brave young Colonel Shaw, who found a grave there, and his heroic men, some dead beneath the walls." Knowing that the Confederates threatened to enslave captured black soldiers, she predicted that some prisoners were "doomed, doubtless, to a fate far, far worse than death."

After a quiet voyage, the *Fulton* approached New York. "Came in sight of land today and this afternoon had a lovely sail up the beautiful harbor, with its stately shipping and fair green islands on every hand...." Charlotte knew that, as a child, Shaw had moved to Staten Island with his family and that his parents still lived there, on a hill overlooking New York Harbor. "Staten Island seemed to me particularly beautiful."

At sunset, the *Fulton* docked in the East River. "There was a great crowd collected on shore. How odd it seemed to see so many white faces! It seems strange to me to be in a great city again. The Southern dream is over for a time. The real life of the Northland begins again— Farewell!"

"She was always young"

Following her return to New York, on August 2, 1863, Charlotte spent a night in the city, then went home to Philadelphia. The August heat was so intense that she went straight to Bucks County, where she wrote a long and thoughtful letter to Shaw's mother. She said in part, "It is not strange that I, belonging to that unhappy race for whom he gave his life, should have a feeling of deep, personal gratitude mingled with the affectionate admiration with which I, from the very first, regarded him." About Shaw's men she wrote, "I believe that there was not one who would not willingly have laid down his life for him."

Remembering her promise to the young, attractive soldier, Charlotte added, "On one occasion, Colonel Shaw, after witnessing the remarkable 'shouts,' and listening with deep interest to the singing of the people on our plantation, expressed his desire to have some of the hymns, to send home....I was very glad to copy them for him, but had not quite finished them when the regiment was ordered away. I send them to you, thinking you might like to have them, as they were copied for him. I regret very much not being able to write the music, as the airs of many of them are very beautiful and touching. While singing, the people keep perfect time with their hands and feet...."

Hallowell, still recuperating from his wounds, was in Philadelphia, with his family. Charlotte paid a visit to him and found him "much improved, sitting up and looking quite cheerful and happy. Had a very pleasant chat with the Colonel, recalling our southern life, but would not stay long lest I should weary him. His stately mother and sisters were very gracious."

It must have been about this time that Charlotte made a correction in her diary. It was probably in conversation with Ned Hallowell that she learned that Shaw had meant her to take charge of his horses, that no gift had been intended. She made this correction without comment.

On August 18, Charlotte stopped in Boston on her way to Salem. In Boston, she was met at South Station by Shaw's father, Francis Shaw, a small, balding man with a full beard. While Shaw's mother gloried in her son's accomplishment, his father was crushed by the loss of one so close to him. Charlotte's visit with him was as short as her mention of it in her journal. She wrote only that the elder Shaw had "a good, noble face, but very sad."

In Salem, Charlotte visited her friend Mary Shephard. The two women went again to visit Whittier. "The poet was in one of his most genial moods, told much about his early life—a very rare thing for him to do—and was altogether as charming as he could be." Whittier was to remain Charlotte's faithful friend until he died in 1892 at the age of eighty-five.

Charlotte went back to Port Royal in October. In a note about the red brick Baptist church and her reunion with her island friends she wrote, "Went to church. It was very pleasant to see the people gathered together again, and to receive their warm welcome."

She found that both Higginson and Ellen Murray were in failing health. Seth Rogers was no longer in Port Royal, and the ghosts of times gone by cast a pall over what had been for Charlotte an exotic and romantic place.

During her second sojourn in Port Royal she wrote only three short pages in her journal, including a brief account of her final Christmas in the islands. She spent the holiday with a white family

Charlotte Forten, seated on the right. Her husband, Francis Grimké, stands behind her.

named Heacock—a young couple and their child—who ushered her "into a cozy little sitting room, all aglow with the light of a blazing wood-fire." She wrote, "The Heacocks are the pleasantest, cheeriest people...and Annie is the veriest little sunbeam I ever saw."

In March 1864 she received the news that her father had enlisted in the Union army and had been appointed sergeant major of a

Pennsylvania regiment. Two months later, Robert Bridges Forten died of typhoid fever, and shortly after Charlotte heard about his death she left Port Royal for the last time.

Six months after the war ended—at Appomattox Courthouse, in Virginia, on April 9, 1865—Charlotte went to work in Boston, for the Freedmen's Union Commission. While in Boston, she translated a French novel into English and wrote several essays. She spent a year in Charleston, South Carolina, teaching in the Shaw Memorial School, a private institution for exceptional black children, named for the martyred Colonel Shaw, then settled down in Washington, D.C., where she taught in a black high school, worked in the Department of the Treasury, and continued to write poetry and essays.

On December 19, 1878, when she was forty-one, she married the Reverend Francis Grimké, who was twenty-eight years old. Grimké, born a slave, had overcome all manner of adversity and was soon to become a distinguished minister, educator, writer, and champion of civil rights.

Born on the Grimké plantation, in South Carolina, he was the son of Henry Grimké, an aristocratic planter, and Nancy Weston, one of Grimké's slaves. When Francis—called Frank—was three years old, his father died. He and his brothers lived as free children until 1860, when their white half brother, E. Montague Grimké, threatened to re-enslave them. Afraid that he might be sold, Frank ran away from the plantation and joined the Confederate army, where he served as a valet. When he went home for a visit, his white half brother ordered that he be imprisoned. In jail he grew sick and was sent home, where his mother nursed him back to health, after which his half brother sold him to another army officer.

Following the surrender of the Confederate armies and the freeing of the slaves, Frank and his brother Archibald went north and, with the help of their white half sisters Sarah Grimké and Angelina Grimké Weld, went to college. Frank studied law at Howard University, then decided to become a minister.

Charlotte married Frank Grimké in the year in which he graduated from Princeton Theological Seminary and took up his duties at the 15th Street Presbyterian Church, in Washington, D.C. Their marriage was a loving, happy union. Their only child, Theodora Cornelia, was born on New Year's Day 1880, when Charlotte was forty-two, but died less than four months later.

During a four-year stay in Jacksonville, Florida, where Frank served as pastor of the Laura Street Presbyterian Church, Charlotte wrote the last entries in her journal. They were brief but touching and revealing. She and Frank lived in a four-room house, with orange trees in its front yard. Charlotte wrote of her husband's dedication to his work and, on their seventh wedding anniversary, wrote about her baby daughter's death, saying that her years with Frank would have been the happiest in her whole life "had it not been for that great sorrow! Oh my darling, what inexpressible happiness it would be to have her with us today. She would be nearly six years old, our precious New Year's gift, and how lovely and companionable I know she would have been." In trying to come to terms with her greatest tragedy, Charlotte revealed a developing religious nature. "But I must not mourn. Father, it was Thy will. It must be for the best. I must wait."

In Florida, and later back in Washington, Charlotte kept on writing, mostly poetry and essays, about her people in New England, about a gathering of veterans of the Civil War, about nature and the arts. She and Frank cultivated a friendship with Frederick Douglass, and she wrote an essay about a visit to his house in Washington. Her work was sometimes beautiful, but never quite as fluent or as touching as the best parts of her journal.

Charlotte was justly proud of her husband, a founding member of the NAACP (the National Association for the Advancement of Colored People), who spoke and wrote forcefully in support of that pioneering organization. As debate developed between the gentle and conservative black educator Booker T. Washington and black civil rights activist and social scientist W. E. B. Du Bois, Charlotte and her husband expressed their impatience with conservatism. They gave support, both moral and financial, to the founding of new schools and colleges for black students. Frank served forty-five years on Howard University's board of trustees.

On July 22, 1914, Charlotte died in her house in Washington. Frank was devastated by her death. He wrote, "She never grew old in spirit. She was always young, as young as the youngest." He said that she had charming manners. "She was always thoughtful, always considerate, never allowing the thought of self to intrude or interfere with the comfort and happiness of others." He called his wife "one of the sweetest, loveliest spirits that ever graced this planet."

Acknowledgments

Thanks to the John Simon Guggenheim Foundation for funding early work on this project.

I was, for several years, a student in Philadelphia, Pennsylvania, and have vivid recollections of the city, including the neighborhood where the Forten family lived. These memories, together with information given to me by scholar Julie Winch, made it possible for me to avoid extensive work in archives in Philadelphia. Winch, who is herself at work on a definitive biography of Charlotte Forten Grimké's grandfather, James Forten (1766–1842), was kind enough to read and criticize my manuscript.

I owe a special note of thanks to my allies in South Carolina. At St. Helena's Penn Center of the Sea Islands, I was welcomed as a friend and colleague by Executive Director Emory S. Campbell and the members of his staff. Especially generous were Freda Thompson, Walter Mack, and Faith Brown. Thanks also to Freda Mitchell of the United Community for Child Development, to Dennis Adams at the Beaufort County Library, and Barbara Gilley, present owner of The Oaks, who permitted me to explore her house and its immediate surroundings.

In Washington, D.C., Esmé Bhan, at Howard University's Moorland-

Spingarn Research Center, was a bright and happy source of information, as was Kate McDonough, at the Manuscripts Division of the U.S. Library of Congress.

Thanks to Jim Francis and Dale Neighbors at the New-York Historical Society and to Howard Dodson and his staff at the Schomburg Center for Research in Black Culture, a division of the New York Public Library.

In Boston, Cambridge, and Salem, Massachusetts, friends, colleagues, and librarians gave me enthusiastic help. At Boston's Massachusetts Historical Society, Chris Steele helped me round up photographs, while Donald Yacovone gave me a variety of pointers. Thanks to Norman Tucker of the Boston Athenaum. Esmé Bhan, who was for a time a Fellow at Harvard University's W.E.B. Du Bois Institute, introduced me to several members of that organization who, in turn, gave me information and encouragement. The staff at Harvard University's Houghton Library has helped me consistently, in this and other efforts.

In Salem, at the Essex Institute's James Duncan Phillips Library, William LaMoy pointed me toward information without which I could not have sorted out the geography of Salem or the locations of the city's schools. Also helpful were Park Historian John Frayler, at the Salem Maritime National Historic Site, and archivist Glenn Macnutt, at Salem State College, which, prior to 1932, was the Salem Normal School.

While I was writing this biography, I made almost constant use of the Williams College Sawyer Library. Thanks partly to my friend Frederick Rudolph, who instituted a black studies program at the college in 1965, the Sawyer has become an important source of material on black history. Thanks to Librarian Phyllis Cutler, Assistant Librarian Jim Cubit, and the other members of their staff, especially Lee Dalzell, Peter Giordano, Walter Komorowski, Helena Warburg, Jo-Ann Irace, Linda Hall, Shirley Fitzpatrick, and Susan Lefaver. Thanks also to Robert Volz, Custodian of the Williams College Chapin Library, for providing me with primary information about fugitive slave Anthony Burns.

Two scholars I have never met played vital roles in the writing of this book. These were Gloria Oden, who made an exhaustive study of Forten's early journals and the people mentioned in them, and Brenda Stevenson, who transcribed and annotated all of Charlotte Forten Grimké's journals.

Bibliography

In writing this account of Charlotte Forten Grimké's early life, I quoted often from her journals. To avoid unnecessary complications, I refer in the text to all of Forten's sometimes disjointed entries as her "journal"—singular. Forten's journals first appeared in print in 1953, cut drastically and with an introduction by Ray Allen Billington. This work, which appeared in subsequent editions, was thoroughly discredited in 1983, in Gloria Oden's *The Journal of Charlotte Forten: The Salem and Philadelphia Years Reexamined*, published in volume 119 of the Essex Institute Historical Collections. Brenda Stevenson's complete and responsible transcription of the journals and her introduction to the work were published in 1988.

The letters of Robert Gould Shaw were published privately and may be found at Harvard University's Houghton Library and the New York Public Library. Shaw's wartime letters, edited and with an introduction by Russell Duncan, were published in 1992. At Harvard University's Houghton Library, I discovered a transcript of Forten's letter to Shaw's mother, Sarah Blake Sturgis Shaw.

Aside from general works, newspapers, diaries, and letters, my two most important sources were books by W.E.B. Du Bois and Willie Lee Rose, one of which is a Philadelphia social history and the other a delightful narrative concerning what was called The Port Royal Experiment. Both are listed in the following abbreviated bibliography.

BOOKS:

Brooks, Van Wyck. *The Flowering of New England, 1825–1865.* New York: E.P. Dutton & Co., 1957.

Brown, William Wells. *The Rising Son; or The Antecedents and Advancement of the Colored Race*. Boston: A.G. Brown & Co., 1874.

Burchard, Peter. *One Gallant Rush*. New York: St. Martin's Press, 1965.

———. *We'll Stand by the Union*. New York: Facts on File, Inc., 1993.

Douty, Esther M. *James Forten, the Sailmaker: Pioneer of Negro Rights*. Chicago: Rand McNally, 1968.

Du Bois, W.E.B. *The Philadelphia Negro: A Social Study*. New York: Benjamin Blom, 1967.

Forten, Charlotte L. *The Journals of Charlotte Forten Grimké*, edited by Brenda Stevenson. New York: Oxford University Press, 1988.

———. *Two Black Teachers During the Civil War*. New York: Arno Press, 1969. (Contains *Life on the Sea Islands* by Charlotte Forten.)

Franklin, John Hope. *The Emancipation Proclamation*. Garden City, Doubleday and Co., 1963.

Garrison, William Lloyd. *The Letters of William Lloyd Garrison*, edited by Walter M. Merrill and Louis Ruchames. Cambridge: Belknap Press of Harvard University Press, 1971–1981.

Higginson, Thomas Wentworth. *Army Life in a Black Regiment*. East Lansing: Michigan State University Press, 1960.

Maloney, Joan M. *Salem Normal School 1854–1905: A Tradition of Excellence*. Acton: Tapestry Press, 1990.

Scott, John Anthony and Robert Alan. *John Brown of Harpers Ferry*. New York: Facts on File, Inc., 1988.

Shaw, Robert Gould. *Letters*. Cambridge: Cambridge University Press, 1864.

Stowe, Harriet Beecher. *Uncle Tom's Cabin: or Life Among the Lowly*. Boston: John P. Jewett and Co., 1852.

Whittier, John Greenleaf. *The Letters of John Greenleaf Whittier*. Cambridge: Belknap Press of Harvard University Press, 1975. Edited by John B. Pickard.

———. *The Complete Poetical Works of John Greenleaf Whittier*. Boston: Houghton Mifflin & Company, 1985.

Wilson, Edmund. *Patriotic Gore: Studies in the Literature of the Civil War*. New York: Oxford University Press, 1962.

Winch, Julie. *Philadelphia's Black Elite: Activism, Accommodation and the Struggle for Autonomy, 1787–1848*. Philadelphia: Temple University Press, 1988.

Index

Page numbers in **boldface** refer
to illustrations.